The Truman Administration and China, 1945-1949

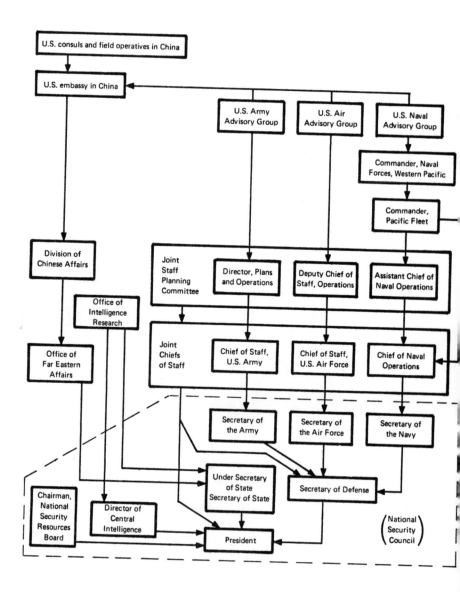

Ernest R. May

Harvard University

The America's Alternatives Series

Edited by Harold M. Hyman

The Truman Administration and China, 1945-1949

J. B. Lippincott Company
Philadelphia/New York/Toronto

ISBN 0-397-47328-1
Library of Congress Catalog Card Number 74-31184
Printed in the United States of America

1 3 5 7 9 8 6 4 2

Library of Congress Cataloging in Publication Data

May, Ernest R.
    The Truman administration and China, 1945-1949.

    (The America's alternatives series)
    Bibliography: p.
    Includes index.
    1. United States—Foreign relations—China.
2. China—Foreign relations—United States. I. Title.
E183.8.C5M38   327.73'051   74-31184
ISBN 0-397-47328-1

To Dorothy Borg

Contents

Foreword

"When you judge decisions, you have to judge them in the light of what there was available to do it," noted Secretary of State George C. Marshall to the Senate Committees on the Armed Services and Foreign Relations in May 1951.[1] In this spirit, each volume in the "America's Alternatives" series examines the past for insights which History—perhaps only History—is peculiarly fitted to offer. In each volume the author seeks to learn why decision makers in crucial public policy or, more rarely, private choice situations adopted a course and rejected others. Within this context of choices, the author may ask what influence then-existing expert opinion, administrative structures, and budgetary factors exerted in shaping decisions? What weights did constitutions or traditions have? What did men hope for or fear? On what information did they base their decisions? Once a decision was made, how was the decision-maker able to enforce it? What attitudes prevailed toward nationality, race, region, religion, or sex, and how did these attitudes modify results?

We freely ask such questions of the events of our time. This "America's Alternatives" volume transfers appropriate versions of such queries to the past.

In examining those elements that were a part of a crucial historical decision, the author has refrained from making judgments based upon attitudes, information, or values that were not current at the time the decision was made. Instead, as much as possible he or she has explored the past in terms of data and prejudices known to persons contemporary to the event.

Nevertheless, the following reconstruction of one of America's major alternative choices speaks implicitly and frequently explicitly to present concerns.

[1] U.S. Congress, Senate, Hearings Before the Committees on the Armed Services and the Foreign Relations of the United States, *The Military Situation in the Far East* 82d Cong., 2d sess., Part I, p. 382. Professor Ernest R. May's "Alternatives" volume directed me to this source and quotation.

In form, this volume consists of a narrative and analytical historical essay (Part One), within which the author has identified by use of headnotes (i.e., Alternative 1, etc.) the choices which he believes were actually before the decision makers with whom he is concerned.

Part Two of this volume contains, in whole or part, the most appropriate source documents that illustrate the Part One Alternatives. The Part Two Documents and Part One essay are keyed for convenient use (i.e., references in Part One will direct readers to appropriate Part Two Documents). The volume's Part Three offers users further guidance in the form of a Bibliographic Essay.

From the climactic military victories of 1945 to the startling détente of 1972, a foreign policy question of high concern for many Americans involved the proper relationship of their nation to China. Professor Ernest May reviews here the reasons for this preoccupation of Americans with China and the outworking of this concern in the formative years after World War II. His analysis and conclusions, based upon the most relevant and insightful documentary sources, open doors to the past through which History has brought us to our present relationships with mainland China. The opportunity to pass with him through these doors allows insight from hindsight, and sharp perceptions are always wanted.

Harold M. Hyman
Rice University

Acknowledgments

An abridged version of the Introduction was presented as one of the Louis Martin Sears memorial lectures at Purdue University in February 1974. I am grateful to the History department of that university for the opportunity and to students and guests of the university for their comments. Through the good offices of Professor Charles Neu, I was able to present yet another abridged version of the essay as the Marjorie Harris Weiss lecture at Brown University, and I am equally in debt to the audience there for their questions and suggestions.

I am also grateful to friends and colleagues who were kind enough to read one draft or another of the Introduction, particularly Dorothy Borg, Warren I. Cohen, Robert Dallek, John K. Fairbank, Charles S. Maier, and James C. Thomson, Jr. In addition, I want to thank the following members of the Faculty Seminar on Bureaucracy, Politics, and Policy of the John F. Kennedy School of Government at Harvard, who devoted an afternoon to forcing from me a defense of the theses in the Preface: Francis Bator, William M. Capron, Thomas Garwin, Philip Heymann, Albert O. Hirschman, Anne Karelekas, Richard E. Neustadt, Don K. Price, Gregory Treverton and Harry Weiner.

Finally, I want to thank Mary Ellen Gianelloni for typing and retyping the various drafts of this work; and the series editor, Harold Hyman, for his imaginative and tolerant supervision.

Part One

The Truman Administration and China

Introduction

Referring to literature, T. S. Eliot once observed that a student "will not find it preposterous that the past should be altered by the present as much as the present is directed by the past." The point strikes any student of contemporary history, for we often have in our minds images of events a decade or a few decades in the past, thinking them as fixed as cutout silhouettes, only to find that, as other events intervene, they change like shadows.

Truman's China policy is a case in point. For fifteen to twenty years after Mao Tse-tung overthrew Chiang Kai-shek, it seemed an unquestionable truth that the United States had thereby suffered a major setback in the Cold War. For the student of United States history, the only interesting question was why the American government had not acted to prevent it. The best known scholarly work on the subject was entitled *America's Failure in China*.

The passage of another decade, with the American war in Vietnam and an American-Chinese détente, has changed the history on which we look back. Our puzzlement is different. Now, we are disposed to ask: how did the United States escape entrapment in China? Why were the Chinese spared the ministrations we later visited on the Vietnamese?

Perhaps another question to be posed is why the United States, after failing to intervene in China, should have sent military forces into Korea in 1950. The issues in China and Korea were so different, however, that the two cases do not lend themselves to comparison. For the American government saw itself in 1945—49 as deciding whether or not to take part in a civil war between armed political groups in a single Asian nation. Rightly or wrongly, American officials saw themselves in 1950 as facing a situation in which one sovereign nation had committed aggression against another, crossing a recognized international frontier. The fact that both parties spoke Korean seemed as irrelevant as the fact Germans and Austrians both spoke German at the time when Hitler seized Austria in 1938. The question was not whether to assist one Korean faction against another but whether to uphold the Charter of the United Nations organization and defend the principle of collective security. There was very little parallelism between debates on China in 1945—49 and debates on Korea in 1950. On the other hand, the perceived issues in China in 1945—49 and in Vietnam in 1961—65 were arrestingly similar.

In both instances, the framers of policy assumed that the spread of Communism menaced the peace and well-being of the world and the national security of the United States. Within a year or so after World War II, President Truman and his principal advisers had become convinced that the Soviet Union and international communism were as threatening as had been Germany and nazism. Though a policy of opposing Communist expansion was first proclaimed in the Truman Doctrine of 1947, a commitment to carry out this policy, even at the price of war, had already been agreed upon within the administration. It was reaffirmed and made more emphatic during each of a succession of apparent crises, and it was disclosed in confidence to leaders and committees of Congress during hearings on various proposals for economic and military aid to friendly governments. At least by 1947—48, Truman and the men around him held a Manichaean conception of the world not unlike that held a decade and a half later by Kennedy, Johnson, and their associates.

3

These American policy makers regarded the Chinese Communists as instruments of the Soviet Union. This was not a mental reflex, as were later perceptions of all Communists as instruments of an international conspiracy; it was a considered verdict.

Alternative 1

1945: A United, Democratically Progressive, and Cooperative China

Reportage from China

Ever since the mid-1930s, American journalists had been investigating the Chinese Communists. Many had sought specific evidence of links with Russia. For the most part, they reported finding no Soviet agents or advisers in Yenan, the Chinese Communist headquarters, or even Soviet supplies and equipment in Chinese Communist hands. Many characterized the Chinese Communists as independent in leadership and doctrine—perhaps not Stalinist Communists at all.

American government agents in China were, on the whole, more circumspect. During the war, the United States maintained an embassy and a military mission in Chungking, the temporary Chinese Nationalist capital. The head of the military mission served both as commander of American forces in the China theater and as chief of staff to Generalissimo Chiang Kai-shek, the head of the Chinese Nationalist government. A few military officers, intelligence agents from the Office of Strategic Services (OSS), and foreign service officers acted after 1944 as an observer group in Yenan, reporting to the military mission. Like most of the journalists, they found the Communist leaders more attractive than their counterparts in the Nationalist regime. In *Americans and Chinese Communists* (Ithaca: Cornell University Press, 1971), Kenneth E. Shewmaker offers the plausible explanation that the Communists, being materialists and modernizers, were more understandable than the formalistic and traditionalistic Nationalists. With few exceptions, however, American officials in Yenan perceived the Chinese Communists as adherents of Leninist Marxism, sympathetic, if not necessarily subservient, to the Soviet Union. While some of them concluded that the United States would be wise to support the Communists, their chief argument was that the Communists would eventually overcome the Nationalists and dominate China; and if the American government failed to woo them, it would force them into dependence on Russia.

The United States had an alliance, however, with the Nationalists. In 1943 President Roosevelt had arranged a conference at Cairo so that Chiang Kai-shek could meet with him and British Prime Minister Winston Churchill as an apparent equal. Roosevelt had an embarrassingly firm commitment to China's being one of the "big four" which, along with Russia, would guarantee the postwar peace. Hence, the disposition in Washington was to urge unification of Nationalist and Communist armies and, in the longer run, absorption of the Communists into a unified Chinese government (see Document 1-a). This effort eventually involved appointment of a new American ambassador, Major General Patrick J. Hurley, a flamboyant Oklahoma politician more noteworthy for energy and self-confidence than for acumen, and a new American military chieftain, Lieutenant General Albert C. Wedemeyer.

As a result of visits to Moscow and Yenan as well as conferences amid the vases, paintings, silk screens, carpets, and polished teakwood tables of Chiang Kai-shek's elegant offices, Hurley convinced himself that an accommodation, uniting the two armies and incorporating the Communists into a single political system, was within easy reach. When it continued to elude his grasp, he became impatient and angry. He interpreted it as his mission to support Chiang, and after Roosevelt's death, no one in Washington was prepared to instruct him differently. When he found officers of his embassy reporting accommodation to be less likely than he believed and urging that the United States not commit itself to Chiang, he became enraged and charged that anti-Nationalists in the mission and in the State Department were subverting American policy.

Because of Hurley's complaints, most of the foreign service officers who had intimate knowledge of the Communists were transferred to posts outside of China. OSS agents and military officers who had been in Yenan were also dispersed. Even so, Hurley's sense of frustration grew. A few months after the Japanese surrender, he suddenly resigned, declaring to the press that State Department careerists had undone his work.

In fact, the American diplomatic and military missions in China had by then been cleansed of practically every person prepared to consider the Chinese Communists potentially independent of Moscow. The new chief of staff in the embassy was Walter S. Robertson, an efficient, courtly, but provincial Virginia investment banker who had served with Hurley earlier in the war and who was sufficiently anti-Communist to qualify later as assistant secretary for Far Eastern Affairs under President Eisenhower's dogmatically anti-Communist Secretary of State, John Foster Dulles. For the most part, others assigned to China were men not likely to draw fire from Hurley. Like Robertson, they were uncontaminated by previous acquaintance with China.

Many of the new men were, however, foreign service officers who prided themselves on accurate reportage. In setting forth observed facts, they made clear that Soviet advisers, arms, and supplies were still not in evidence among the Communists. They also pointed out that Russian occupying forces seemed to be seizing all movable goods in Manchuria and sending them home rather than turning them over to Chinese allies. Nevertheless, there was little in their dispatches to stimulate doubts about the closeness of Chinese Communists to the Soviet Union. Nor was there much to offset warnings from U. S. military and naval officers and from the U. S. embassy in Moscow that the Russians planned to use the Chinese Communists as instruments for controlling some or all of China.

The Policymakers in Washington

In Washington, this official reportage was screened in the Department of State. Being a more orderly man than his predecessor, Truman curtailed the independence of OSS and other organizations upon which Roosevelt had relied. He directed that information about foreign affairs come to him through the State Department. This did not, of course, stop other agencies from gathering data so that their chiefs could dispute with the State Department. Truman's decree did, however, give officers of the State Department authority which they had not had for some time. If understood and believed by the secretary and under secretary of state, the officers' estimates of situations abroad were more likely than not to be accepted as bases for decisions on policy.

In the department, reports from China went to the Division of Chinese Affairs. Since this division was part of the Office of Far Eastern Affairs, appraisals of what was going on in China went from the chief of the division to the director of the office. In the normal chain, the director then transmitted his evaluations to an assistant secretary of state. (As the department was then organized, one assistant secretary had cognizance of political affairs in Latin America, while one oversaw the rest of the world.) They then went to the under secretary or secretary, or both.

During the first half of 1945, while the war was still going on, the chief of the Division of Chinese Affairs was John Carter Vincent, a gracious but sharp-tongued Georgian who had spent most of his diplomatic career in China and had been number two man in Chungking under Hurley's predecessor. His staff, though small, was heterogeneous, including both critics and supporters of Chiang. Vincent himself was relatively open-minded. He did not have a high opinion of the Nationalist leadership. On the other hand, he took it for granted that the Communists were at least subject to Soviet influence. Like Hurley, he cherished hope that the Russians would encourage the Communists to come to terms with the Nationalists in order to avoid a Soviet-American conflict in Asia.

In mid-1945, Vincent moved up to become director of the Office of Far Eastern Affairs. James F. Byrnes, a former senator from South Carolina, onetime Supreme Court justice, and wartime "assistant president" under Roosevelt, had just become secretary of state and had chosen Dean Acheson as under secretary. Formerly an assistant secretary in the department, Acheson had had a falling out with the Japan hands who previously superintended the Far Eastern Office. Not by nature a forgiving man, he removed these men as soon as he had power to do so, and Vincent was his choice for the succession. Thereafter, Acheson and Byrnes dealt directly with Vincent rather than having him report through the assistant secretary to whom he was nominally subordinate.

Vincent's former job as Chief of the China Division meanwhile went to Everett Drumwright. An old China hand with close ties to missionaries who were fiercely anti-Communist and pro-Chiang, Drumwright was *persona grata* to Hurley. Indeed, Hurley singled out Drumwright by name as the one State Department careerist to have backed him up.[1] After September 1, 1945, when Drumwright effectively took over the division, its memoranda reflected his attitudes. An example is a communication of mid-November which went to Acheson via Vincent. It declared that Communist success in any part of China would "bring about a situation . . . little different from that obtaining before the defeat of Japan. Instead of a Japanese-dominated puppet regime we should probably find in its place one dominated by the U.S.S.R." (see Document 1-b).

Others in the department contributed reports and memoranda which buttressed those from Drumwright. The embassy in Moscow cautioned against any optimism about Soviet cooperation in the Far East. Intent on teaching Truman and his aides to be less naive than their predecessors about Communist ambitions and tactics, officers in the Division of Eastern European Affairs prophesied Soviet use of the Chinese Communists as "an effective machine to build upon and expand their influence in a somewhat similar manner to the methods they have used in central and eastern Europe."[2] At least as early as the end of 1945, there seemed to be consensus in the State Department that the Chinese Communists were acting in behalf of Moscow.

No other department or agency challenged this estimate. Since Hurley's protests had caused reassignments of military as well as diplomatic personnel, American army officers in Manchuria and North China collected evidence of Soviet support for the Communists rather than evidence of Communist independence; and the new military attaché in Chungking filed reports on the "Communist menace." From marine commanders in North China and fleet commanders supporting them offshore came reports of similar tenor. On the basis of intercepted communications shown to him, a Treasury representative in China cabled back information of a Soviet plan to "lie low" for a short period and then, by means of the Communists, seize control of the country. Hence the chiefs of staff and the secretaries heading the War, Navy, and the Treasury departments simply seconded the appraisal made by Acheson and Byrnes on the basis of information passed along by Drumwright through Vincent. In sessions of Truman's cabinet, the only people who questioned this appraisal were Secretary of Commerce Henry A. Wallace, formerly Roosevelt's vice-president, and Secretary of Labor Lewis Schwellenbach. Although Wallace had visited China in 1944 as a special emissary for Roosevelt, neither he nor Schwellenbach possessed current information comparable to that of others at the table (see Document 1-c).

It can thus be said that, by an early point, the Chinese Communists were perceived by American officials much as were North Vietnamese Communists in the 1960s. They were regarded, in effect, as the agents of an outside power.

For a time, it is true, hope persisted for peaceable understandings with the Communists. Policy thinking retained molds from World War II. When preoccupied by the war with Japan, officialdom had defined America's objective as "a united, democratically progressive, and cooperative China which will be capable of contributing to security and prosperity in the Far East." Incorporated in instructions to agents in the field, interdepartmental memoranda, and public speeches by high officials, these phrases served as foundation stones for a complex, interlocking structure. They could not be changed or moved without dismantling much that had been built upon them. Hence, though postwar circumstances were very different, these objectives in policy survived unaltered (see Documents 1-a, 2-a, and 2-c).

Notes

1. U.S., Congress, Senate, Committee on Foreign Relations, *Investigation of Far Eastern Policy*, 79th Cong., 2d sess., 1945, published in U. S., Congress, Senate, Committee on Foreign Relations, *United States-China Relations*, 92d Cong., 1st sess., 1973, Appendix, p. 146.

2. U. S., Department of State, *Foreign Relations of the United States* (Washington, D.C.: Government Printing Office, 1861—), vol. 7, 1945, pp. 982—84, 864. (Hereafter referred to as *FRUS*.)

Alternative 2

Mediation to Achieve Unification: General Marshall's Mission to China

Growing Sentiment for Support of the Nationalists

When they learned, to their surprise, of General Hurley's resignation as ambassador to China, Truman and his associates were not tempted to question the goal of support to Chiang that Hurley had been asked to pursue. Their immediate concern was to defend against the charges from Republicans and admirers of Chiang that they had given Hurley inadequate backing.

The news came while the president was lunching with his cabinet. His reactions indicated both the persistence of past beliefs and the emergence of new ones. According to Secretary Wallace's diary, Truman "said we were the only big nation that wanted a united democratic China. The President said that unless we took a strong stand in China, Russia would take the place of Japan in the Far East." The secretary of agriculture suggested that the president respond by asking General George C. Marshall, the wartime army chief of staff and a national hero, to take over Hurley's assignment. Truman accepted the suggestion and acted upon it that afternoon (see Document 1-c).

When the Senate Foreign Relations Committee subsequently held hearings on Hurley's resignation and Marshall's nomination as special representative of the president, Secretary of State Byrnes testified that America's aim was "a strong, united, and democratic China." This language was then quoted in Truman's formal instructions to Marshall.[1]

It was understood that Marshall would go to China to carry on what had been begun during the war. He would try to get the Nationalists and Communists to compose differences, allow the merger of their armies into a single nonpolitical national army, and agree to compete peacefully within some mutually acceptable constitutional system. In order to get Nationalist concessions, Marshall was empowered to use almost every form of enticement or threat. There were more than 100,000 American troops in China, mostly marines. They had helped Chiang's forces move from south China to north

China and Manchuria. By controlling certain ports and railroads, they kept open Nationalist supply lines and freed Nationalist troops for other purposes. Marshall could offer to keep the American forces in place or threaten to withdraw them. Similarly, he could offer to release or withhold relief funds and military supplies still being shipped in fulfillment of wartime commitment. Finally, he had authority to tell Chiang that the United States would support him if the Nationalists were reasonable and the Communists were not, and that it would desert him if the Communists were reasonable and the Nationalists were not.

Although Marshall dutifully accepted the president's commission, he insisted that Truman and Byrnes look at the possibility that the stated objective of the United States would prove unobtainable. He asked if the president and secretary of state did not agree that, if the United States actually abandoned Chiang, "there would follow the tragic consequences of a divided China and of a probable Russian reassumption of power in Manchuria, the combined effect of this resulting in the defeat or loss of the major purpose of our war in the Pacific." According to Marshall's notes, "The President and Mr. Byrnes concurred in this view of the matter" (see Document 2-a).

For reassurance, Marshall obtained from Truman and Undersecretary Acheson a secret codicil to his instructions—"that in the event that I was unable to secure the necessary action by the Generalissimo, which I thought reasonable and desirable, it would still be necessary for the U. S. Government, through me, to continue to back the National Government of the Republic of China . . ." (see Document 2-b). Thus, even though the United States adhered to the wartime definition of objective, there was already a high-level consensus that the American government should back *any* non-Communist regime in China against Communist opponents. This was not unlike the consensus in the early 1960s about Vietnam.

From December 1945 to January 1947 Marshall labored for Chinese unification. He held interminable meetings with Nationalist and Communist negotiators. To bring the Nationalists into line, he made ruthless and effective use of the powers delegated to him. For a brief period, he secured a truce. But the arrangement collapsed; fighting resumed, and Marshall finally despaired and asked that the president recall him. By that time, Truman had already decided to dispense with Byrnes and put Marshall in his place. So Marshall returned to the United States in early 1947 to become secretary of state.

Notes

1. U. S., Congress, Senate, Committee on Foreign Relations, *Investigation of Far Eastern Policy*, 79th Cong., 2d sess., 1945, published in U. S., Congress, Senate, Committee on Foreign Relations, *United States-China Relations*, 92d Cong., 1st sess., 1973, Appendix, p. 96; U. S., Department of State, *United States Relations with China with Special Reference to the Period 1944—1946* (Washington, D.C.: Government Printing Office, 1949), pp. 764—814. (Hereafter referred to as *The White Paper*.)

Alternative 3

Military Aid to Nationalist China

The Diplomats' Perspectives

When Marshall came back to Washington, he felt that the contingency he had foreseen in 1945 was actually coming to pass. He blamed his failure in China less on the Communists than on the Nationalists. The intractability of Chiang had continually irked him. The cliques in control of the ruling Kuomintang party had seemed to him both reactionary and corrupt, and he had been outraged by the refusal of the Nationalist leaders to adopt reforms that would attract popular support away from the Communists or even to institute changes that might make their armies better able to fight (see Document 2-c). As secretary of state he had to face the issue of whether, given these circumstances, the United States should support the Nationalist regime.

The American diplomatic mission in China was virtually united in urging such support. Although Marshall had had plenary powers in China, he had not carried the title of ambassador. Robertson had acted as chargé d'affaires until mid-1947, when John Leighton Stuart was named as Hurley's successor in the embassy. A New Testament scholar, and formerly a Presbyterian missionary in China, Stuart had been president of the Yenching University of Peiping. He had all the attitudes of a bearer of the white man's burden, viewing the Chinese with a mixture of impatience, affection, and zealous optimism. He would point out to Washington that the Chinese had a "lack of self-reliance . . . partially accounted for by the family system and other age-long patterns," and that there was a "chinese trait of denouncing some other person for one's own mishaps." At the same time, he would profess confidence "in the capacity of the Chinese people to master modern techniques and to acquire truly democratic standards of public morality." He once reported of a conversation with Chiang: "I told him that . . . the greatest help that America could give was not money nor military advice but the dynamic force of our ideals. . . ."

Although Stuart acknowledged and deplored defects in the Nationalist regime, he had affection for Chiang (who was a Christian convert), and he had little doubt that the United States ought to guarantee Chiang's survival and success. He viewed the Chinese Communists as wholly tied to Moscow and, in any case, as "cruelly authoritarian." There was in progress a "struggle between Communists and democratic ways of life," he believed, and the Chinese Communists were on one side while the Nationalists and the United States were on the other. To aid Chiang's regime, he declared in a cable to Washington, "is the delicate but splendidly creative opportunity for American statesmanship."[1]

In Stuart's opinion, the Nationalists needed more than material aid, and more even·than exhortation to adopt American ideals. As a practical matter, he felt, they needed tutelage, guidance, and direction. Sketching what he had in mind, he once instanced "American-directed army reorganization," American training for the armed forces, "qualified American advisers and auditors" in the railway system, and participation by American firms and government agencies in the development of industry. Chiang, he reported, "has recognized with cold realism the inherent weaknesses of his country both human and material and has disciplined himself to paying the price for American monetary aid in having it accompanied by a large measure of American control" (see Document 3-d).

Those who knew Stuart were aware of his independence. Working mostly in his residence, he seldom visited the embassy, and he relied more on the Chinese secretary whom he had brought from Yenching University than on any of his official aides. Foreign service officers in the mission viewed Stuart with misgivings not only because he was a noncareerist ·and because they suspected his secretary of being an agent for Chiang, but also because, as one of them wrote, Stuart "had learned how to be just as oblique and, when necessary, just as devious as any Chinese."[2]

The embassy, left quasi-autonomous by Stuart, was supervised first by Robertson and subsequently by W. Walton Butterworth, another newcomer to the Far East but, in contrast to Robertson, a career diplomat. Butterworth sometimes communicated to Washington opinions of the mission which did not coincide with Stuart's.

Butterworth and some of his junior colleagues regarded Stuart as excessively pro-Chiang. Indeed, in 1946, Butterworth urged Marshall not to give up and go home, saying "that he felt General Marshall's departure would be catastrophic, and in view of Dr. Stuart's inclinations, would cause the United States, as far as its policy is concerned, to drift toward full support of the National Government."[3]

No less than Stuart, however, Butterworth and most of his colleagues felt it important that the Communists not prevail. Halting aid to the Nationalists, they advised the department, "would ultimately result in a chaotic condition in which the Chinese would find themselves at the mercy of Soviet machinations." They differed from Stuart in arguing more strongly that political and economic reforms should be demanded as the price of American aid. They also differed with the ambassador in regarding Chiang as a liability rather than an asset. By 1948 officers of the diplomatic mission were engaged in clandestine efforts to encourage replacement of the Generalissimo by one of two members of the Kwangsi clique—either General Li Tsung-jen, the allegedly more liberal Nationalist vice-president, or Marshal Li Chi-shen, who headed a Kuomintang Revolutionary Committee based in Hong Kong.[4]

Dispatches to Washington from Stuart and his underlings resembled very closely dispatches from Saigon in the early 1960s in which some members of the United States mission championed full support of Ngo Dinh Diem while others criticized Diem and advised helping one or another of the Vietnamese generals who would eventually depose and murder him. Nearly all the American diplomats in China advocated aid for the Nationalists and predicted that, given favorable circumstances, aid could prevent Communist success.

The Military's Perspectives

For the most part, American military and naval officers in China argued even more ardently for aiding the Nationalists. Partly because of general postwar demobilization and partly because of decisions made by Marshall, American forces in China were reduced from over 100,000 to around 6,000. Once most of the Japanese forces in China had been rounded up and shipped back to Japan, General Wedemeyer's China Theater Command was deactivated. Meanwhile, however, Wedemeyer and other officers developed plans for a postwar Army Advisory Group and Navy Advisory Group. When shown these plans, Vincent protested that they envisioned "a de facto protectorate with a semi-colonial Chinese army under our direction." At Vincent's urging, Byrnes signed a memorandum objecting to the proposed advisory groups. The War and Navy departments then scaled them down and limited their functions (see Documents 2-a, 3-b, and 3-c). Nevertheless, by mid-1946, about 1,000 American military and naval personnel were assigned to advising Chiang and his commanders on how to run the Nationalist armed forces.

Heading the Army Advisory Group was Major General John P. Lucas, a West Point graduate who had been a corps commander in the Italian theater. Like his wartime predecessors in China, he judged the Chinese to be potentially excellent soldiers who needed only to be equipped and trained, to learn how to care for their weapons, to be paid regularly, and to be deployed and led by commanders who knew what they were doing. If Washington would give him authority and wherewithal, Lucas felt sure, he and his advisory group could build a first-rate army and defeat the Communists. He estimated that he could do the job in about two years, if the United States would provide arms and supplies equivalent to those needed for ten American divisions and if he could more or less control Chinese strategic and operational planning (see Document 5-a).

Brigadier General John P. McConnell headed an almost autonomous section of Lucas's command, advising on military aviation. Having served in Southeast Asia and China during the war, he had more background than Lucas, and his reports to Washington described the Nationalist air force as being in pitiable condition. Nevertheless, he advised that that force could rapidly be made efficient and effective, if it were only suitably equipped and trained.

The Naval Advisory Group had as its chief Rear Admiral Stuart S. Murray, who had commanded submarines in the southwest Pacific during the war. His reports to Washington warned in the strongest terms of the strategic advantage which the Russians would gain if the Chinese Communists won control of any part of China and if the United States could not have a base at Tsingtao. Like Lucas and McConnell, he advocated aid to the Nationalists accompanied by supervision of military training, plans, and operations.

Murray's recommendations to Washington were powerfully seconded by Admiral Charles M. Cooke. Commanding the Seventh Fleet, "Savvy" Cooke was the senior American officer in the region. He had been the navy's chief planner in World War II, and his nickname indicated his reputation. When Marshall was in China, Cooke fought unsuccessfully against reductions in the marine forces there. He argued persistently that loss of the Tsingtao base would be catastrophic, and he urged on Washington a variety of schemes for training Chinese marines and for using United States naval forces to aid the Nationalists.[5]

All in all, American military and naval representatives in China were probably as ardent advocates of military aid as were their counterparts in Vietnam a decade and a half later; and their estimate of the utility of relatively limited American involvement was much more optimistic. American military men in Saigon during the early 1960s reckoned success in Vietnam as likely to take ten years rather than two and to require much larger quantities of both equipment and American personnel. The similarities, however, are more striking than the differences, for both groups forecast dire consequences if the United States did not act, and both exhibited utter confidence that American technology and know-how could determine the outcome of an Asian civil war.

In Washington, the fate of recommendations from the missions in China depended as much on the military establishment as on the State Department. In part, this was because military aid was at issue. In part, it was because civilian policy makers had respect for and confidence in their military advisers. Roosevelt had deferred to Marshall and the other chiefs of staff more than to any others in his entourage. Though Truman tried initially to make himself less dependent on the professional military, State Department staff work disappointed him, and he felt compelled to turn to the Pentagon. His selection of Marshall as secretary of state evidenced both his esteem for the professional military and his persisting uneasiness about reliance on military agencies. Even so, he respected the judgment of his service secretaries and of chiefs of staff such as Eisenhower and Omar Bradley, and continued to listen to them.

The Bureaucratic Structure of Military Decision Making

In fact, in 1947 the involvement of the military establishment in policy making was formalized through legislation. Concerned primarily with the organization of the military establishment, this legislation created a Secretary of Defense and provided for a separate air force. Although there had been agitation to do so, the act did not create an overall chief of staff for the three services. Instead, it gave formal existence to the Joint Chiefs of Staff, previously an ad hoc committee, consisting of the three uniformed service heads (the chiefs of staff of the army and air force and the chief of naval operations) and the chief of staff to the commander in chief (at this time, Fleet Admiral William D. Leahy), who served as liaison with the President. Also, the legislation of 1947 established a National Security Council with the secretary of state, secretary of defense, and civilian service secretaries as members. The existence of this council was supposed to ensure that foreign policy decisions not be made without consideration of military implications.

The positions of the military establishment on issues of foreign policy were developed by complex processes. In the army, the critical body was the Plans and Operations Division of the General Staff. After the spring of 1947, its chief was Wedemeyer. He advised both the army chief of staff and the secretary of the army on all policy issues.

The navy had a more complex organization. There, various sections of the office of the chief of naval operations divided up work on policy questions. Since major commands in the navy were not yet subject to centralized control such as that of the general staff in the army, the staff units in Washington deferred to the various fleet headquarters. In the case of Admiral Murray's proposals, the basic evaluation was thus made in the Seventh Fleet under the eyes of Admiral Cooke. Officers in Washington introduced amendments only after consultation with the fleet headquarters. It was thus Cooke who guided the chief of naval operations and his deputies and, through them, the secretary of the navy.

The collective position of the Joint Chiefs resulted from negotiations between army and navy staff officers and their counterparts in the air force, for the key committee of the Joint Chiefs consisted of Wedemeyer and his opposite numbers from the other services. Agreements among these officers produced papers which would be approved, usually with relatively little change, by the chiefs of staff. Since the civilian service secretaries and the secretary of defense had almost no other advisers on issues such as aid to China, they, too, were likely to accept the views of the planners as communicated to them through individual chiefs of staff or collectively by the Joint Chiefs.

From records currently available, it is not easy to reconstruct military staff work on the China aid issue. Since documents signed by the chiefs of staff or the civilian secretaries all expressed views congruent with those of Wedemeyer and Cooke, one can infer that they were pivotal. They gave cues to the junior officers who collected and appraised data. They then marketed the resultant reports and memoranda to their peers and superiors in the services. Apparently, no one in the military establishment was prepared to contest the belief of Wedemeyer and Cooke that Communist victory in China would have grave consequences for the United States and that the Nationalists should therefore be given military aid as proposed by Lucas, McConnell, and Murray:

that is, aid which entailed American training and American supervision of Chinese plans and operations.

The service staffs also had officers, however, who were concerned about other theaters, particularly the Middle East and Western Europe, where Communist takeover seemed even more imminent. Moreover, Eisenhower, Bradley, and the successive air force chiefs of staff all tended to regard Europe as more important to the United States than Asia.

As a result, staff processes produced in the spring of 1947 a memorandum by the Joint Chiefs asserting that Communist victory in China could produce "very grave long-range jeopardy to our national security interests" but assigning China relatively low priority as a claimant for American military aid.[6]

Toward the end of the same season—on June 9, 1947—the Joint Chiefs signed another memorandum seeming in some respects to contradict what they had said earlier. Concerned only with China, it had passed through fewer editorial hands and bore more of the impress of Wedemeyer and Cooke. In it, the chiefs said categorically that the Chinese Communists "are tools of Soviet policy" and that "the military security of the United States will be threatened if there is any further spread of Soviet influence and power in the Far East." Hence, the chiefs recommended "carefully planned, selective and well-supervised assistance to the National Government, under conditions which will assure that this assistance will not be misused." Spelling out the implications of this recommendation, they said that the United States should give up the policy of not interfering in the civil war. Preserving some consistency with their earlier opinion about China's priority, they offered the hope, however, that "even small amounts of United States assistance to the National Government will materially strengthen its morale and at the same time weaken the morale of the Chinese communists" (see Document 3-e).

The civilian secretaries at the head of the military service departments felt very much as did the uniformed Joint Chiefs. Earlier in 1947 the secretary of war had questioned whether the United States should adhere to the policy of staying out of the Chinese civil war. James V. Forrestal, secretary of the navy and then the first secretary of defense, listened sympathetically to naval officers who championed a larger American role in China. On more than one occasion, he argued to Marshall that the United States should make a major effort to set Nationalist China on its feet.

The chiefs of staff and the civilian secretaries were more sanguine about China than their counterparts would be later with regard to Vietnam. In 1961, for example, the Joint Chiefs were to advise that effective aid to Diem was likely to require committing more than 200,000 American combat troops, and Secretary of Defense Robert McNamara was to transmit this advice to the president.[7] In 1947 the chiefs reckoned requirements in China as minimal. When pressed to be more specific, they turned to Wedemeyer, and he came up with a figure of 10,000 officers and men as the probable American force necessary to give Chiang victory.[8]

The State Department's Perspectives

In the State Department, the China experts were skeptical about these estimates. In July 1946 Drumwright had been given a choice overseas assignment, the first secretaryship in London. His place as chief of the Division of Chinese Affairs went to Arthur Ringwalt, and Philip Sprouse came back from the mission in China to be Ringwalt's deputy. Both Ringwalt and Sprouse had served under Vincent in Chungking during the early part of the war. They saw more nearly eye to eye with him than had Drumwright.

Memoranda from the China Division or from Vincent himself as director of the Office of Far Eastern Affairs consistently warned against overoptimism. In regard to the June 9 recommendations of the Joint Chiefs, for example, Vincent wrote to Marshall, "it is the opinion of the Far Eastern Office that a USSR-dominated China is not a danger of sufficient immediacy or probability to warrant committing ourselves to the far-reaching consequences which would ensue from our involvement in the Chinese civil war on the side of the National Government" (see Document 3-f).

While the China Division and the Office of Far Eastern Affairs were primary advisers for the top officers of the department, they were not the only ones. At the time there was still in progress a bureaucratic battle which would eventuate in creation of a separate Central Intelligence Agency. Many survivors of the wartime Office of Strategic Services were temporarily in the fold of the State Department. They were grouped in special, separate units. Eyed askance by foreign service officers, they were, to the greatest extent possible, kept in subordination by the regular geographic divisions. Nevertheless, there were China specialists in the Office of Intelligence Research, and they succeeded on at least one occasion in getting to Secretary Marshall their estimate of what rescuing Chiang would entail—$2 billion in economic aid over a two-year period plus equipment for thirty to sixty Chinese divisions (see Document 5-b). The intelligence analysts were thus more pessimistic than the military establishment in calculating costs. Unlike Vincent and the foreign service China hands, however, they took the view that military aid to Chiang deserved consideration.

More audible voices were those of the other geographic divisions. Although the social rules of the department inhibited one bureau's taking issue with another about affairs in the other's part of the globe, the preeminent Office of European Affairs took care to pass on to the secretary all cables from Moscow which reported Soviet support for the Chinese Communists. When occasion offered, officers in the European and Middle Eastern branches probably conveyed subtly their opinion that Vincent and his colleagues lacked sufficient appreciation of the ruthlessness of the Soviets and the magnitude of their ambitions. Although the department was dominated by European-oriented foreign service officers, the prevailing opinion within it, as army liaison officers observed in 1946, was that "we should preserve a position which will enable us affectively to continue to oppose Soviet influence in China. . . . It is felt that failure to maintain this position would have the gravest effect on our long-range security."[9] Outside Vincent's Office of Far Eastern Affairs, attitudes within the State Department tended to resemble those within the military establishment.

Among later civilian bureaucrats who dealt with Vietnam, there was a comparable line-up. By that time, the Central Intelligence Agency was not only independent but large and influential, and the intelligence community contained most of the government's Southeast Asian experts. While much more guarded in policy advice than Vincent and his associates had been, these intelligence analysts made quite plain their skepticism about the probable effectiveness of American intervention in Vietnam. They were counterbalanced, or more than counterbalanced, by civilians in their own agencies and elsewhere who were expert on other areas of the world but also assigned high importance to the American stake in Vietnam and assumed blithely that, if there were a will to win there, a way would be found to do so.

Notes

1. *FRUS*, vol. 7, 1945, pp. 26, 29—30, 101, 105—7, 115—17; *FRUS*, vol. 7, 1948, p. 367.

2. John F. Melby, *The Mandate of Heaven: Record of a Civil War, China 1945 49* (Toronto: University of Toronto Press, 1968), p. 137.

3. *FRUS*, vol. 10, 1946, p. 575.

4. *Ibid.*, p. 148; *FRUS*, vol. 7, 1948, pp. 52—268; Melby, *Mandate of Heaven*, p. 268.

5. For estimates by McConnell, Murray, and Cooke, see *FRUS*, vol. 7, 1947, pp. 73—80, 864—61, 944—45, 953; and testimony by Cooke, U. S., Congress, Senate, Committee on the Judiciary, Internal Security Subcommittee, *Hearings on the Institute of Pacific Relations*, 81st Cong., 1st and 2d sess., 1949—50, pp. 1492—1515.

6. *FRUS*, vol. 1, 1947, p. 745.

7. *The Pentagon Papers*, Senator Gravel Edition, 4 vols. (Boston: Beacon Press, 1972), vol. 2, pp. 108—9.

8. U. S., Congress, Senate, Committee on Armed Services and Foreign Relations, *Hearings on the Military Situation in the Far East*, 82d Cong., 1st sess., 1951, p. 465. Unfortunately, no documentary evidence of Wedemeyer's 10,000-man estimate has yet come to light. We remain dependent on Marshall's recollection, uttered almost four years after the fact.

9. *FRUS*, vol. 10, 1946, p. 28.

Alternative 4

Military Advisors for Nationalist Forces: General Wedemeyer's Mission to China

"Moral Encouragement and Material Aid"

A crucial factor in America's relationship to China in 1947 was the leaning of Secretary of State Marshall. Experience in China had convinced him that the Chinese Communists were "playing the Russian game," but it had also persuaded him that Chiang's regime was incompetent. When the military establishment first began to press for aid, he responded that he was not yet sure whether it was necessary or desirable, but he implied that, if there were a program, it would entail close American supervision. Even the granting of credits, he said, should probably be accompanied by an economic advisory mission with "more authority than is implied in the word 'Advisory.' "[1]

Reports from China in the first half of 1947 were uniformly depressing. The Nationalists' advantage in manpower seemed to be diminishing; Communist forces were growing in size and improving in morale; and there were gloomy predictions that Nationalist units might defect. Chiang's hold on cities in Manchuria seemed to become more and more precarious, and Stuart warned that the Nationalists might not even be able to hold northern China (see Document 3-d). Reading bulletins from the embassy, the military mission, and American reporters, Marshall grew more and more worried about a possible Nationalist collapse. Yet the weaknesses of Chiang's regime showed no sign of being remedied. Briefing a group of businessmen in early June, Marshall said candidly, "I have tortured my brain and I can't now see the answer."[2]

The Joint Chiefs' memorandum recommending aid to Chiang reached Marshall at about the time when he was adjusting to a new under secretary. Acheson had agreed to remain for six months. Visibly exhausted, he left office on June 30. His successor, who began taking over during the preceding month, was Robert A. Lovett, a Wall Street banker who had come to know Marshall when assistant secretary of war for air during World War II. He was the equal of Acheson in acumen and his superior in personal finesse.

Almost as soon as Lovett was formally installed, Marshall confided to him the trend in his thought about China. He agreed with Vincent, he said, that the Joint Chiefs' advice was "not quite realistic. . . . Nevertheless," he went on, "the situation is critical and it is urgently necessary I feel that we reconsider our policy to see what changes may be necessary. . . ." Marshall had not decided what, if anything, to do; but he had selected a procedure for deciding. Unless Lovett saw reasons for not doing so, he proposed to ask Wedemeyer to revisit China and then to recommend a course of action for the government (see Document 3-g).

This decision by Marshall invites speculation. It is possible that Marshall settled on Wedemeyer as simply the best man for the job; Wedemeyer had been one of his principal staff aides during the early part of the war and had been helpful to him in China. Moreover, Wedemeyer knew Chiang and other Chinese leaders. Since Marshall was aware of Wedemeyer's opinions, however, it is also possible that he selected him because he himself was leaning toward intervention and wanted a recommendation to that effect. On the other hand, Marshall was not a guileless man. He believed, he once told Acheson, in "not antagonizing people but managing them."[3] Conceivably, Marshall regarded Wedemeyer as a man who could be managed. He may have hoped to get from him a report which would counsel against military involvement. If so, he would have a stout club to use against the missions in China, the chiefs of staff, the service secretaries, and other "hawks." At least at the present time, it is impossible to judge which of these hypotheses is the more plausible.

Lovett concurred in the plan. Marshall then arranged for Wedemeyer's appointment as special representative of the president. He allowed the general to draft his own instructions, but amended them so that they did not categorically promise "a program of rehabilitation and stabilization provided the Chinese Government stipulates, guarantees and accepts definitive supervisory measures to be maintained by representatives of the United States." Instead, Wedemeyer was advised that the United States "can consider assistance in a program of rehabilitation only if the Chinese Government presents satisfactory evidence of effective measures looking towards Chinese recovery and provided further that any aid . . . shall be subject to the supervision of representatives of the United States Government" (see Document 4-a).

Accompanied by a small staff, Wedemeyer made a month-long tour, visiting not only the Nationalist capital but also Formosa, Canton, Shanghai, and areas in the north and northeast. Soon after arriving, he reported to Marshall that conditions had grown worse since Marshall's departure. The Nationalists seemed to him "spiritually insolvent." After touring regions where the civil war was hotly in progress, he commented cynically that the Nationalists would do all they could to get the United States to fight their war. He was not disposed, however, to wash his hands of them. Rather, he wrote, "we must . . . compel them to make realistic contribution in the global effort first to retard, then stop Soviet aggressions, and later to penetrate peacefully through political, economic and psychological means those areas within the Soviet orbit."[4]

Leaving China, Wedemeyer went to Hawaii to prepare a report. The instructions which he gave to the drafting officers indicated that his basic views remained unchanged. He said that he wished to recommend "moral encouragement and material aid," and that he wanted direct American supervision. Commenting that he desired a program comparable to that in Greece, he implied that he wished military assistance by supervision of plans and operations. The one new element in Wedemeyer's thought was a notion that Chiang should be relieved of responsibility for Manchuria. He had concluded that Chiang had little chance of retaining a foothold there. The remedy which occurred to him was that the United States seek establishment of a United Nations trusteeship comparable to that in Korea. If it came into being, some Soviet forces could return, but American, British, and French forces would also come in. Manchuria could then be turned into a buffer zone, and Nationalist troops which might otherwise be committed there or on the Manchurian borders could be released to fight the Communists elsewhere (see Document 4-b).

The final report which Wedemeyer delivered to Marshall and the president on September 19 included a strong recommendation for United Nations action in Manchuria. It was, he argued, "necessary to prevent that area from becoming a Soviet satellite." In addition, he urged large-scale economic aid, accompanied by close supervision; military aid in the form of vehicles, weapons, ammunition, aircraft, and transport vessels; and an expanded role for American military and naval advisers. Though Wedemeyer stopped short of proposing that these advisers accompany Nationalist units in the field, he said that they should "provide advice *indirectly* to tactical forces" by carrying out reconnaissance missions, determining which units should remain in combat and which should be withdrawn for retraining, and directly supervising training, outfitting, and the maintenance of services of supply.[5]

Again, there is a striking parallel with later events, for Kennedy's decision in 1961, like Marshall's in 1947, was to dispatch a special mission. Kennedy, like Marshall, chose a military man whom he respected, whom he knew to have hawkish propensities, but whom he probably thought that he could manage. This was General Maxwell Taylor, a former army chief of staff whom Kennedy had brought out of retirement to serve as special assistant in the White House. The one noteworthy difference was that, whereas Marshall equipped Wedemeyer with a political adviser of Vincent's persuasion (Sprouse of the China Division), Kennedy named as civilian coleader of the mission to Vietnam Walt Rostow, a White House aide already known as an advocate of military intervention. Still, Kennedy's tactics and Marshall's seem remarkably similar; and the outcome was much the same. For Taylor and Rostow also suggested a disguised method of introducing United States forces to stabilize a deteriorating situation. Their proposal was that the troops go in allegedly to assist in flood relief. Like Wedemeyer, they went on to urge expanded economic and military aid, extensive American supervision, and enlargement of the military advisory mission to include reconnaissance, training, and supply, but not direct involvement in combat.[6]

We do not know either what Marshall hoped of Wedemeyer or what Kennedy desired of Taylor and Rostow. Whatever was Marshall's expectation, Wedemeyer's report evidently did not satisfy it. The recommendation for a United Nations trusteeship for Manchuria certainly came as an unwelcome surprise. At the same time, the American missions in Greece were reporting hopefully about progress in defeating the Communists; and Marshall foresaw that publicity for Wedemeyer's proposal might lead to agitation by Communist states for United Nations takeover of Greece. Worse still, it could revive debate in Congress, where some key members had already criticized the Greek-Turkish aid program for being unilateral rather than United Nations-sponsored. Hence, after failing to persuade Wedemeyer to debate the recommendation on Manchuria, Marshall decided to treat the document as a top secret advisory report, to be shared with as few people as possible and not to be communicated even in summary to Congress or the press.

Notes

1. John F. Melby, *The Mandate of Heaven: Record of a Civil War, China 1945—49* (Toronto: University of Toronto Press, 1968), p. 98; *FRUS*, vol. 7, 1947, p. 808.

2. David E. Lillienthal, *Journals: The Atomic Energy Years, 1945—1950* (New York: Harper and Row, 1964), p. 201.

3. Dean G. Acheson, *Present at the Creation* (New York: W. W. Norton, 1969), p. 216.

4. *FRUS*, vol. 7, 1947, pp. 682—84, 712—15, 725—26.

5. U. S., Department of State, *The White Paper*, pp. 764—814.

6. *The Pentagon Papers*, Senator Gravel Edition, 4 vols. (Boston: Beacon Press, 1972), vol. 1, pp. 87—98, 652-54.

Alternative 5 ════════

════════ Intervention
in the
Chinese
Civil War

Public and Congressional Pressures for Aid

The months following Wedemeyer's mission formed an anxious period for Marshall, but with China only occasionally surfacing as a central concern. Shortly before receiving Wedemeyer's report, he had been told that "all indications point towards a major political showdown crisis between the Soviet Union and the non-Soviet world. . . . It is not a matter of several years in the future. It is more likely a question of months." His staff pinpointed Western Europe as the probable theater for a Soviet offensive. Not until November did Marshall's planners begin to assure him that war was not in sight. They prophesied, however, that the Soviets would probably take over Czechoslovakia (which occurred six months later) and attempt to foment civil wars in Italy and France.[1] It was not a time when the secretary had much leisure for further torturing his brain about China.

Marshall faced, however, increasing pressure to do something for Chiang. The diplomatic and military missions in China and the military establishment in Washington were unrelenting. With Wedemeyer's backing, Lucas came up with detailed plans for training ten Chinese divisions (see Documents 5-a and 5-c). The new Department of the Air Force urged enlarging the air advisory mission and providing more planes; and Cooke presented schemes for turning over additional quantities of supplies to the Nationalists and for developing and training a Nationalist marine corps.

Meanwhile, public agitation mounted for aiding Chiang. Henry R. Luce had taken up the cause in 1946. The son of missionary parents and himself brought up in China, Luce felt passionately that Chiang, the Christian convert, merited support by the United States. His widely circulated news and picture magazines, *Time* and *Life*, passed up no opportunity for editorializing or slanting reportage so as to enhance the image of the Nationalists and blacken that of the Communists. In the autumn of 1947, Luce commissioned and gave wide publicity to "China: A Report to the American People" by William C. Bullitt, a former ambassador to the Soviet Union and to France and a onetime intimate of President Roosevelt. In the "Report," Bullitt warned that Russia was on the verge of taking over China and declared, "The independence of the United States will not live a generation longer than the independence of China" (see Document 5-g).

Roy Howard of the United Press and the Scripps-Howard newspaper chain joined Luce's campaign. So did William Randolph Hearst, Robert R. McCormick of the *Chicago Tribune*, Eleanor Patterson of the *New York Daily News*, and other publishers who had consistently been anti-Red and critical of the Roosevelt and Truman administrations for emphasizing interests in Europe over those in Asia. Some voices opposed them, most notably those of the left wing weekly, *The New Republic*, and those of reporters who had been in China during the war (see Document 5-f). But the loudest clamor was that set up by Luce and his fellow publishers.

A bloc in Congress also agitated for aid to Chiang. Foremost in its ranks was Republican Representative Walter Judd of Minnesota, who had spent his youth as a Congregationalist medical missionary in China. With assistance from the Chinese embassy and its lobbyists, Judd delivered well-documented and powerfully argued speeches in Chiang's behalf. As an expert on China, he made his influence felt on the rest of the House Foreign Affairs Committee. Officers such as Wedemeyer and Cooke meanwhile made converts of members of the House Armed Services Committee. A junket to China and long interviews with Chiang and other Nationalist leaders confirmed their faith. While there was no counterpart to Judd on the Senate side of the Capitol, the persuasive powers of Nationalist agents, coupled perhaps with campaign contributions, did make a zealot out of Styles Bridges of New Hampshire, the senior Republican on the Appropriations Committee.[2]

Through 1946 there had been voices on Capitol Hill challenging those of Judd and Bridges. Indeed, Byrnes and Acheson had been fearful lest public and congressional opposition prevent the United States from even helping Chiang to move troops into parts of China disputed with the Communists. The progress of the Cold War had tended since then to still editorial writers who questioned active opposition to international communism; and the overwhelming Republican victory in Senate and House elections of 1946 removed from Congress most of those who had been outspokenly critical of Chiang. Hence, in the fall of 1947 Marshall and his associates were mostly reading and hearing public and congressional commentary that paralleled advice from Stuart, Lucas, Wedemeyer, and the military services. Meeting with the Chinese ambassador in November, Marshall acknowledged a "wave of sentiment in favor of aid to China."[3]

In confronting these pressures, Marshall no longer had Vincent by his side to articulate the counterarguments. In 1945 Vincent had been attacked by Hurley. Criticism of him was voiced time and again by partisans of Chiang, Chinese Nationalist officials, and probably in private by both military officers and hard-line foreign service officers. And once Acheson left, Vincent no longer had a protector. According to Foreign Service rules, he was due for rotation to an overseas assignment. Marshall chose not to bend the rules but to send Vincent off as minister to Switzerland and bring Butterworth back from China to take his place.

Butterworth had fewer misgivings than Vincent about an American commitment to prevent Communist victory. He remained skeptical, however, as to the wisdom of betting on Chiang. His memoranda therefore did not challenge the principle of American involvement in the civil war. They did prod the secretary and under secretary to ask searching questions about the probable effectiveness of specific measures proposed.

With Marshall and Lovett preoccupied with Europe, the mission and the military establishment putting in proposal after proposal, partisans of Chiang agitating outside, and the Far Eastern experts in the department giving only cautionary advice, piecemeal decisions set an apparent trend toward eventual all-out aid to the Nationalists. Before the dispatch of Wedemeyer to China, Chiang and his supporters had stressed their need for ammunition, arguing that the United States had given them weapons but now denied them cartridges and shells. The American military attaché reported that, in fact, no one knew whether ammunition was in short supply or not, because the Nationalists had no system of inventories.[4] Nevertheless, Marshall approved arrangements for the Chinese to buy American ammunition. During the autumn, he agreed to subsidize some arms purchases and release to the Chinese certain United States stockpiles in the western Pacific.

Theretofore, provision of military equipment had been rationalized as merely fulfillment of a wartime pledge to outfit China with thirty-nine divisions and eight and one-third air groups. In his earlier effort to extort concessions and reforms from Chiang, Marshall had halted delivery of this equipment. Now, in October 1947, he agreed that the remaining supplies to round out these forces be rushed to China.

At the beginning of November, Marshall crossed a line by authorizing the Army Advisory Group to commence on Formosa a limited training program for Chinese combat forces. He also approved enlargement of the advisory group's mission. Following Butterworth's advice, he reserved judgment on some of its proposals, but he gave a go-ahead for its proceeding to reorganize and supervise the Nationalist army's services of supply. Meeting with the secretary of defense and the service secretaries, Marshall described the position to which he had come. Everyone now agreed, he said, "that we wish to prevent Soviet domination of China." Though still deploring the character of Chiang's regime, the United States had no choice but to keep it in power. Marshall "said that the immediate problem is to determine what we can do effectively" (see Documents 5-c, 5-d, and 5-e).

Here, parallelism with later policy making on Vietnam ceases to be so exact, for Kennedy allowed the substance of the Taylor-Rostow report to leak into the press. Furthermore, he made a single decision rather than a series of little decisions. Accepting in essence the recommendations of Taylor and Rostow, he dispatched ten thousand American troops to serve as advisors in Vietnam. It can hardly be said, however, that at this point the two histories plainly part company, for the drift in the Truman administration seemed to be toward a commitment comparable to that later made by Kennedy.

Notes

1. *FRUS*, vol. 1, 1947, pp. 763-65, 770-71.
2. See Ross Y. Coen, *The China Lobby in American Politics* (New York: Macmillan, 1960), p. 62.
3. *FRUS*, vol. 7, 1947, p. 1215.
4. Ibid., pp. 8-9, 13-14, 464-66; U. S., Department of State, *The White Paper*, pp. 989-90.

Alternative 6

A Policy of Non-intervention

Aid to China and Europe: Limiting Considerations

It was in the winter of 1947—1948 that United States policy toward China became definitely one of nonintervention. At the end of 1947, the Nationalists still had more troops than the Communists. They had not lost Manchuria, as had seemed likely at the time of Wedemeyer's visit. By mounting a counteroffensive, they had pushed the Communists back in some areas. Although ceding more and more of the countryside in Shantung, Hopei, and Shansi provinces, they retained control of most of the cities and rail lines in north China. In a much publicized but militarily insignificant campaign, they captured the now deserted Communist headquarters at Yenan. Most of the Yangtze valley and all of China to the south remained free of Communist forces. No one looking at crude statistics and battle maps had reason as yet to regard the Nationalist cause as hopeless.

The American diplomatic mission in China insisted, however, that the Nationalists' military position was at "a critical state." Lewis Clark, a foreign service officer who had served in China from 1926 to 1935 but had subsequently been in Paris and Ottawa, succeeded Butterworth at the embassy. He filed a dispatch in December which asserted that "measures taken to guard against a Government military collapse must be adopted promptly;" that military supplies alone would be of no use, whatever their quantity; and that it was essential for American officers effectively to take over central military planning and to ensure the implementation of their plans through liaison units with the Nationalist field commands. Stuart and the embassy united in reiterating and reemphasizing this recommendation, and it was warmly seconded by Lucas, Murray, and Cooke in the Far East, and by Wedemeyer and other military and naval planners in Washington (see Documents 5-a and 5-c).

Heading the administration's agenda at the time was the Marshall Plan for Europe. To carry it forward, the administration estimated a need to spend $17 billion over the next four years, more than a third of it during the coming eighteen months. The president summoned Congress into special session to consider the necessary legislation. But the act had to pass through Styles Bridges's Senate Appropriations Committee; and it was obvious from the outset that Bridges would take the occasion to press for aid to China.

Bridges did so. He called Wedemeyer as a witness and elicited from him public testimony to the effect that China was as important to the United States as Europe; that economic and military aid was urgently needed by

Chiang; and that any such aid should be accompanied by close supervision. Bridges also provided a forum for Judd and for Alfred Kohlberg, the principal Nationalist lobbyist. From Bullitt, Bridges obtained headline-making testimony disclosing the recommendations coming from the United States embassy in China and urging, as in his "Report to the American People," that General Douglas MacArthur, the wartime army commander in the southwest Pacific, now supreme commander in occupied Japan, and long an idol for American conservatives, be sent to take command of Chiang's armies (see Documents 6-a and 6-c).[1]

State Department witnesses before Bridges's committee did not offer battle to Wedemeyer and the others. They simply pleaded for prompt aid to Europe, promising a specific proposal for aid to China in the near future. Bridges was not satisfied, nor were his counterparts on the House Appropriations and House Foreign Affairs committees. It became evident that the administration would not get aid to Europe without aid to China.

In the State Department, study of an aid program for China had been under way since the autumn of 1947. As with preparation of the Marshall Plan, the work fell to specialists on economic affairs rather than to the regional officers. For China, as for Europe, the economic planners thought primarily of enabling the recipient country to rebuild productive capacity and to finance imports without balance of payments deficits. They hardly thought at all of military needs.

When finally consulted, the Far Eastern specialists were not altogether unhappy with the result. Pointing out that both the Congress and the Chinese would be particularly concerned about imports of munitions, they suggested to the economic planners that China's prospective earnings from exports be underestimated by about $50 million in order to allow Chiang that amount for purchases of military supplies. The alternative would be a special appropriation for military assistance, wrote Butterworth to the assistant secretary for Economic Affairs, and "the consequences of the adoption of such a program by the U. S. Government are too serious and too obvious to require elaboration."[2] The department sent to Capitol Hill a proposal for a one-year appropriation of $570 million for economic aid to China.

Marshall and Lovett recognized that this proposal would not satisfy Bridges and those who thought as he did. They were uncertain as to what would be the upshot. Arrangements were already in progress to reassign Lucas and install as head of the Army Advisory Group Major General David G. Barr, who had been on Eisenhower's staff in Europe during World War II. Stuart and others argued that the change should not be made without an accompanying change in directive which assured that Barr could render "effective aid." Marshall's own preference by this time was plain. If he had earlier had any inclination to consider intervention, it had disappeared. As he indicated to Stuart, he feared "acceptance of responsibility for a military campaign with its inevitable international perils and probable tremendous demands of one kind or another." But he could not gauge accurately the will of Congress, and thus held to the position that Barr's precise mission would have to be determined later.[3]

The China Aid Act: "Three Cheers for the Nationalist Government"

The proposed legislation for aid to China went first to the House Foreign Affairs and Senate Foreign Relations committees. They had to recommend a bill authorizing appropriations, and the two houses had to act on it. Only after that would the Appropriations committees consider actual funding.

When the Foreign Affairs and Foreign Relations committees met in joint executive session, Marshall stated his own position candidly and vigorously. He could not do so publicly, he explained, because it would hurt Nationalist morale. It was his considered judgment that the Communists could not be wholly overcome by the Nationalists and that, in fact, they might win. For the United States to underwrite the Nationalists would, however, involve "obligations and responsibilities . . . which I am convinced the American people would never knowingly accept." The United States, said Marshall, "would have to be prepared virtually to take over the Chinese government" and to commit "sizeable forces and resources over an indefinite period." He could not estimate the probable requirements, he conceded, but he felt sure that "the magnitude of the task and the probable costs thereof would clearly be out of all proportion to the results to be obtained" (see Document 6-a).

Marshall's testimony did not persuade the House Foreign Affairs Committee. Wedemeyer, Bullitt, and others told its members that limited military aid could be effective. With Judd taking the lead, the committee resolved that some funds should be earmarked for such a purpose. It also voted that United States military advisers should be assigned to China, as to Greece. Its report was adopted by the House.

The Senate Foreign Relations Committee, however, was much more in agreement with Marshall. We now have access to records of that committee's executive sessions. They show that Republican and Democratic members were equally firm in regarding military aid as unwise. Henry Cabot Lodge of Massachusetts told his colleagues, "I will be willing to vote to send them some money, but I'll be damned if I want to send them manpower." Alexander Wiley of Wisconsin expressed a similar view, as did Bourke B. Hickenlooper of Iowa and Elbert Thomas of Utah, the most conservative Republicans in the group. Hickenlooper told his colleagues that he had considered going out to China in the 1920s, just after graduating from law school. He had been assured that great progress was in prospect. So far as he could tell, he said, no progress had in fact occurred during the subsequent twenty years.

Arthur Vandenberg of Michigan, the chairman of the Foreign Relations Committee, summed up the opinion of his colleagues in the observation that the House and Bridges might be appeased by allocating some funds for military supplies but that no responsibility should be assumed for seeing that the funds were spent wisely. The bill, he said, would be "essentially three cheers for the Nationalist Government" (see Documents 6-b and 6-c).

Acknowledged to be one of the two most powerful Republicans in the Senate and facing no opposition on this issue from Robert A. Taft of Ohio, his colleague in Senate leadership, Vandenberg had no difficulty persuading the upper house to follow his guidance. A conference committee of the Senate and House then turned out compromise legislation following Vandenberg's formula. It authorized $338 million for economic support and $125 million for military supplies for China, but it declared that there was no "express or implied assumption by the United States of any responsibility for policies, acts, or undertakings by the Republic of China or for conditions which may prevail at any time." This language was approved by both houses (see Document 6-d).

When appropriations were to be made, Bridges and his counterpart in the House Appropriations Committee, John Taber of upstate New York, revived the issue. Though reducing the sum for economic aid to $275 million, the appropriations act which cleared Taber's committee and passed the House retained $125 million for military aid and stipulated that it be administered under supervision comparable to that for military aid to Greece. Despite Bridges's enthusiasm for Senate acceptance of this provision, Vandenberg and his allies exerted themselves successfully for a Senate bill and conference committee report which omitted it. Like the authorizing China Aid Act of April 3, the final appropriations act registered three cheers for Chiang without committing the United States to do more than give him money.

Marshall's Decision Against Military Involvement

At least by early 1948 Marshall and Lovett had definitely decided on the policy which they preferred. Marshall no doubt continued to be influenced by his frustrating experience in China. The cautious views of Butterworth and the China Division, still manned by Ringwalt and Sprouse, probably carried some weight with both the secretary and undersecretary. So did counsel from George F. Kennan, the Soviet expert heading the Policy Planning Staff, who recommended concentrating on a buildup of Japan and conceded that "there is not much we can do in China." As evidenced by Marshall in his congressional testimony and by Lovett in talks with his good friend, Senator Vandenberg, the secretary and undersecretary had become convinced that the United States should not in any way become engaged militarily in China.[4]

Marshall and Lovett were at first merely advocates of such a policy, disputing the contrary policy views of the missions, the military establishment, and public figures such as Judd and Bullitt. Although Marshall had unique standing with the president and had White House backing in pressing his views on Congress, he apparently did not expect Truman to sustain him if Congress failed to do so. At any rate, until they were reasonably sure how Congress would act, Marshall and Lovett temporized in dealing with questions posed by the military establishment. They kept open the option of enlarging the mandate of the military mission until the outcome of debate in Congress enabled them to insist upon their position. The legislative branch, as much as the executive branch, determined American policy.

Of course, the decision was not taken as final by those who regarded it as unwise. As reports flowed in during 1948 of reverses suffered by Nationalist forces, partisans of Chiang in Congress and the press raised their voices ever louder. Exercising influence in a joint committee set up to keep track of all foreign aid expenditures, Bridges and Taber employed Bullitt as a consultant, sent him to China, and publicized his reports. Henry Luce's publications became more and more shrill in denouncing administration policy.

Meanwhile, the diplomatic and military missions and the military establishment passed up few opportunities to press for reconsideration. The embassy continued regularly to file recommendations that American officers assume a larger role in planning and guiding Nationalist operations. Soon after his arrival in China, General Barr proposed a scheme to this effect more ambitious than any of Lucas's. He was enthusiastically seconded by Admiral Oscar Badger, who had succeeded Cooke as the senior United States naval officer in the western Pacific. Together, Barr and Badger advocated that American officers assume responsibility for operational planning in key Nationalist field commands. In Washington, the Joint Chiefs formally endorsed the issuance of such orders (see Documents 6-e—6-h).

Marshall promptly met with the secretary and undersecretary of the army, the army chief of staff, and Wedemeyer. He said that he had no objections to the Army Advisory Groups' providing limited training well away from combat areas, but he categorically opposed placing any advisers with operational commands. He also insisted that the advisory groups exercise no supervision over Chinese decisions as to what to purchase with the $125 million or what to do with the materiel thus purchased. He said that "the important thing was ... to do this without 'getting sucked in'. ..." On his demand, the proposal by Barr and Badger was vetoed (see Documents 6-g and 6-h).

Time and again thereafter, Marshall or Lovett suppressed similar initiatives. The most embarrassing came from Badger, who proposed that, if the Communists attacked Tsingtao, he would join with the Nationalists in repelling them. The United States had a naval base at Tsingtao by virtue only of an informal understanding with Chiang. In private, Badger confessed that he did not see any valid rationale for retaining it. Officers on his staff and in Washington were nevertheless resolute that, since the United States had the base, it should not give it up. Despite objections from the State Department, the Joint Chiefs gave Badger the orders he requested, and Forrestal backed them up. Only by going to the president did Marshall and Lovett get a ruling that Badger should promptly evacuate Tsingtao, thus eliminating the likelihood that the United States would be drawn into a shooting war alongside the Nationalists.[5]

As late as October 1948, Stuart and other Americans in China still pleaded for American takeover of Nationalist military planning. In a long cable to the ambassador, Marshall reemphasized all the points made eight months earlier in his presentation to the Foreign Affairs and Foreign Relations committees, adding that the latter committee had accepted his reasoning. So far as he was concerned, he indicated, the issue was closed (see Documents 6-i and 6-j).

That almost marked the end. Soon afterward, the bulk of the embassy staff conceded that Chiang's cause was hopeless. Barr, too, had concluded that the Nationalists were finished. The Pentagon reluctantly accepted his estimate. Although the bureaucracy went through the motions of developing a follow-up aid program for China, the higher levels of State and Defense turned to such issues as whether or not to recognize a Communist government if it took control of all of China. So far as available documents indicate, the possibility of lending military backing to Chiang did not again receive serious consideration during the remaining year in which Chiang struggled futilely to retain the mainland.

Although debate was to rage for a decade about what should have been done, real debate about whether or not actually to intervene militarily in China stretched only over the year from the spring of 1947 to the winter of 1947—48. All the time, the alternatives were those specified in the Joint Chiefs' memorandum of June 9, 1947 (see Document 3-e). The United States could either have tried to save Chiang by military aid and advice or, as it did, acquiesce in control of China by the Communists. Some State Department memoranda argued that "conditional aid" was a third option; but in fact, it was not. The phrase merely signified a policy of postponing choice.

Notes

1. U.S., Congress, Senate, Committee on Appropriations, *Hearings on the Third Supplemental Appropriations Bill for 1948*, 80th Cong., 1st sess., 1947, pp. 122-73.

2. *FRUS*, vol. 8, 1948, pp. 442-78.

3. Ibid., pp. 8-9, 13-14; U. S., Department of State, *The White Paper*, pp. 989-90.

4. *FRUS*, vol. 1, 1947, p. 775; U. S., Congress, Senate, Committee on Foreign Relations, Historical series, Memorandum of conversation between Lovett and Vandenberg, 80th Cong., 2d sess., November 4, 1947, pp. 517-18.

5. *FRUS*, vol. 8, 1948, pp. 310-25.

Retrospect

If Vietnam, Why Not China?

The Factual Bases of the Decisions

Despite the resemblance between the China issue of 1945—49 and the Vietnam issue of 1961—65, the policy outcomes were wholly different. Why? For such a large prize as China, why did the Truman administration not make at least a limited military commitment such as Kennedy made in 1961 for the much smaller prize of Vietnam?

One hypothesis belabored by right wing extremists in the 1950s was that a clique of Communists and Communist sympathizers in the executive branch conspired to bring about decisions desired by Moscow. Even when a significant part of the available evidence consisted of documentation and testimony unearthed by congressional inquisitors bent on proving its validity, this thesis seemed unlikely. Now that a large body of sources has become open for research, it seems preposterous.

In the 1950s and afterward, defenders of the Truman administration replied to such charges by arguing that the decisions about China were simply products of rational calculation—decisions which would have been made by any reasonable men similarly situated. This counterhypothesis appeared in two versions. One emphasized the magnitude and complexity of the problem in China. The State Department issued in 1949 a "White Paper"—a large collection of documents relating to American China policy since 1944. The introduction, signed by Dean Acheson, declared: "The unfortunate but inescapable fact is that the ominous result of the civil war in China was beyond the control of the government of the United States. . . . It was the product of internal Chinese forces. . . ." (p. xvi).

The second version emphasized the relative military weakness of the United States at the time. Testifying in 1951, Marshall said:

> My recollection is that at that particular time there were one and a third divisions in the entire United States. I know I was concerned and the Chiefs of Staff were very much concerned over obtaining enough men to guard the air strips at Fairbanks against a possible drop there. . . . There was very little with which to do. When you judge decisions, you have to judge them in the light of what there was available to do it.[1]

The arguments in the "White Paper" and in Marshall's testimony once seemed to provide a convincing explanation. In post-Vietnam retrospect, this no longer seems the case.

One cannot explain the difference in outcome by observing that China was large while Vietnam was relatively small. In the Foreign Relations Committee, to be sure, Senator Lodge remarked that China was distinguishable from Greece because it was "so damned big" (see Document 6-b). But this consideration cut two ways, for there was some correlation between size and importance. Most Americans took it for granted in 1947—48 that if the Communists won China, they would gain something of value. In 1961—65 few regarded South Vietnam itself as a major asset. The rationale for blocking its conquest depended on a domino theory which supposed jeopardy to other countries which could be counted as valuable. China's size should have been as much an argument for intervention as against it.

Nor can one any longer accept the "White Paper" thesis that rescue of the Nationalists was obviously a task "beyond the control of the government of the United States." We now know that the Truman administration's agents in China were advising that the contrary was true. Americans in the field were just about as optimistic as were those in Vietnam in the early 1960s. And if there were voices of caution in 1947—48, there were also such voices in 1961—65. The *Pentagon Papers* show not only that the CIA gave warnings about the probable difficulty of saving South Vietnam but that Secretary of State Dean Rusk cabled President Kennedy in 1961, "I would be reluctant to see U. S. make major additional commitment American prestige to a losing horse."[2]

In 1947—48 and in 1961—65 policy makers in Washington were offered both encouraging and cautionary counsel. There was no inherent reason why those of the earlier period should not have decided, like those of the 1960s, to listen to advisers who said that the task was manageable.

Nor is the decision of 1947—48 explicable, as Marshall claimed, as a function of American military weakness. The estimates put before the decision makers in 1947—48 did not describe success in China as beyond American capabilities. In June 1947 the Joint Chiefs formally advised that a very limited American military commitment could reverse the course of events (see Document 3-e). The best-qualified staff officers took the position that ten thousand officers and enlisted men could do the job. Had that number of troops been sent to China, it would have represented less than two percent of the soldiers and marines on active duty. In 1961 Taylor and Rostow recommended sending exactly the same number of men to Vietnam—ten thousand "advisers." The Joint Chiefs, however, warned Secretary of Defense McNamara that acceptance of the Taylor-Rostow recommendations would entail committing more than two hundred thousand U. S. troops to combat.[3] This larger figure represented twenty percent of the ground forces then on active duty.

Although some civilians saw the military recommendations of 1947 as unrealistic, few questioned at the time that the United States could accomplish the desired end if it chose to engage its own manpower. Even Vincent once said that the Communists could be overcome if "we were prepared to take over direction of Chinese military operations and remain in China for an indefinite period."[4]

Members of the Truman administration discounted the optimism of their missions in China and the estimates of their military advisers that China could be rescued through a small commitment of American military power. They chose instead to heed relatively cautious analysts and to assume that the military investment would have to be large. By contrast, members of the Kennedy and Johnson administrations discounted both the pessimism of their Washington-based analysts and military warnings that Vietnam would require a lot of American manpower. If one looks simply at what the two administrations were being told by presumed experts, it is not at all clear why nonintervention should have seemed the rational choice in one instance while intervention seemed the rational choice in the other.

To be sure, there were many contradictory reports and estimates concerning China in public media while there were few such reports or estimates in circulation concerning Vietnam. The later policy makers were much more the prisoners of images conveyed to them through official channels. Even so, it remains difficult to explain the differences in outcome as products of different sets of objective facts.

The Perceptual Bases of the Decisions

As an alternative, it might be hypothesized that the general framework of perception was different in the two periods. This is, in fact, a thesis implicit in many histories which deal with events of 1945—49. These histories portray the United States as having emerged from World War II innocently or idealistically hoping for international cooperation and coming only reluctantly, slowly, and with considerable psychological stress to a perception that the Soviet Union and international communism were forces no less ruthless, aggressive, and menacing than had been the Axis powers. This change is described as not complete until after the Berlin crisis and Czechoslovakian coup of 1948, perhaps not until after the Korean conflict. The issue of whether or not to intervene in China, it would follow, arose too early in the Cold War. The comparable issue concerning Vietnam arose, by contrast, after the Cold War mind-set had fully hardened.

As indicated earlier, this hypothesis is made less compelling by documentary evidence which has come to light in the 1970s. Previously classified files show almost beyond question a consensus by 1946 among bureaucrats, high-level officials, and key legislators that the Soviet Union was a dangerous and predatory foe, that all Communist parties were its instruments, and that the preservation of American values and perhaps of the United States itself depended upon containing the spread of Soviet power and influence. These files also show wide agreement that the Chinese Communists were at least allies of the Russians and that their success in China would be a significant victory for America's Cold War enemy (see Documents 1-b, 3-d, 3-f, 4-b, 5-a, and 5-b).

To be sure, some American officials questioned how much the Russians would gain from a Chinese Communist triumph. Vincent argued that the costs to them might outweigh the benefits. Showing extraordinary foresight, Kennan forecast that the Soviets would face an enormous and intractable problem in controlling a Chinese Communist state.[5] But the sparser documentation on the later Vietnam debate contains comparable memoranda, pointing out difficulties which the North Vietnamese would encounter in trying to govern South Vietnam and suggesting that North Vietnam's Ho Chi Minh might prove "an Asian Tito."

And it is simply not the case that Cold War assumptions were more firmly fixed in the early 1960s than in the late 1940s. After all, members of the Truman administration were completely convinced by 1947—48 that inclusion of Communists in coalition governments led inevitably to Communist takeover. Not only to the public but to themselves, they denied that they had ever desired a Nationalist-Communist coalition in China.[6] They were also sure by 1947—48 that no Communist government could be trusted to keep its word and that purely diplomatic understandings were thus impossible. The Kennedy administration, by contrast, showed willingness to experiment with a coalition government in Laos, and Kennedy and Johnson both carried on the search for détente with the Soviet Union commenced by Eisenhower and later continued by Nixon.

In short, it is probably not the case that the Truman administration chose the alternative it did because members of that administration had not yet accepted the fundamental perceptions and assumptions associated with the Cold War. In economists' language, the relevant preference curves of the Truman administration and the Kennedy and Johnson administrations were not so dissimilar as to account for differences in behavior.

The Economic Bases of the Decisions

Yet another mode of explanation would assume that America's ruling class perceived its interests differently in the two situations. Insofar as one can judge such an explanation by tests of evidence, however, it does not seem persuasive. In gross quantitative terms, the American stake in China was larger than in Vietnam. Not only in percentage of gross national product but in actual dollars, there was more trade with China in 1948 than with South Vietnam in 1961. Though figures are not easily accessible, it is almost certainly the case that American capital investment in China was larger. Furthermore, as historians influenced by Marx have argued, China was visualized by American financiers and businessmen as a huge potential market, the future exploitation of which would be immensely profitable for American capitalism. Records relating to United States economic policy in 1945—49 indicate that this image survived.[7] Nothing of the sort held true for South Vietnam in the 1960s.

Even if one supposes that the policies of a capitalist state are likely to be determined by the special rather than the general interests of the ruling class, it is hard to frame a plausible explanation. For China had the eye not only of special interest groups such as owners of silver mines, growers of cotton, and producers of cotton textiles but also of specific corporations with well-founded reputations for being able to get what they wanted from the government. Sosthenes Behn's International Telephone and Telegraph Company owned public utilities in Shanghai and had aspirations for developing power, light, and communications networks throughout China. Pan American Airways and Trans-World Airlines were in competition for airline routes to and within China, and Pan Am was already in partnership with some high Kuomintang officials in owning the Chinese National Aviation Corporation. Standard Vacuum and the Texas Company were two American oil companies with substantial holdings and ambitious plans in China.[8] If manipulative special interests could have had their wish, one would suppose that ITT, Pan Am, TWA, Stan Vac, Texaco, and their like would have brought about decisions to do whatever was necessary to keep the Nationalists in power.

To be sure, a resolute economic determinist could contend that American capitalists did not uphold Chiang because they thought the Kuomintang party committed to a kind of nationalist socialism almost as antagonistic to "open door imperialism" as the Marxist socialism of the Communists. Complaints by American businessmen about their treatment by the Nationalists could be cited as supporting evidence. By the time of the decisions against military intervention, however, these complaints had died down. From the spring of 1947 onward, the Nationalists were making generous concessions to American investors and entrepreneurs. They signed a commercial treaty with the United States which satisfied every desire of enthusiasts for the open door, and they passed legislation promising to keep at a minimum the government role in the economy.[9] There was nothing in the stance of the Nationalists in 1947—48 to inhibit American capitalists from supporting them to the fullest extent.

In regard to South Vietnam, one has difficulty identifying significant groups or corporations in the United States that stood to lose much if it went Communist or gain much if it did not. It is thus hard to sustain an argument that economic interests dictated military intervention there while they did not dictate it in China. (Indeed, it may be that the line of argument is stronger if reversed: that is, if one supposes that actual economic interests are a disincentive for intervention because they make it harder to rationalize intervention as altruistic.)[10]

The Critical Variables in the Decisions: Psychological Factors

If the differences in outcome in 1945—49 and 1961—65 are not satisfactorily explained by differences in objective facts, or general framework of perception, or economic determinants, how are they to be accounted for? Unfortunately for the social scientist interested in engineering future outcomes, the critical variables were probably interlocking psychological, structural, and environmental factors more or less specific to the two time periods and not likely again to coincide, either by accident or by contrivance. They included the following, which one might classify as psychological factors.

1. *The image of war.* Although there had been limited wars and proxy wars in the past, including a whole series from the Crimean War to the Spanish Civil War, the two World Wars dominated American conceptions of international conflict. Consciously or perhaps more often unconsciously, Americans fancied that if their intervention on the side of the Nationalists led to Russian intervention on the side of the Communists, the result would be an all-out war like that with the Axis powers. Fear of such a war was plainly not an absolute deterrent. Truman accepted the risk of another world war when he intervened in Korea in 1950. In fact, he did so even though suspecting that the Soviets might be trying to divert American forces so that they could attack Europe. Nevertheless, one senses that apprehension of all-out war imposed an extra degree of caution on Truman, Marshall, Lovett, and even on Forrestal and the Joint Chiefs when intervention in China was under debate.

In view of the Soviet development of nuclear weapons, the rocket-brandishing of Khrushchev, the valor and competence shown by Chinese Communist armies in Korea, and the growth of Chinese Communist military power in the intervening decade, Americans in the 1960s should have had more reason to fear conflict. By then, however, they had experienced a major limited war and lived through or observed several episodes in which limited military intervention had not developed into anything larger. Consciously or unconsciously, they could say to themselves: if we go into South Vietnam and don't invade North Vietnam, as we invaded North Korea in 1950, we will run minimal risk of conflict with a major power. The possibility that military intervention might lead to a large-scale war scarcely entered into thinking about Vietnam.

2. *The absence of a warning precedent.* The men who decided China policy in 1945–49 expected some criticism. They did not anticipate the ferocious and scurrilous attack which actually materialized, culminating in 1951 when Senator Joseph R. McCarthy, the most irresponsible of the anti-Communist demagogues, charged Marshall with witting participation in a pro-Communist conspiracy. Certainly, they did not foresee that the manufacturers of such nonsense would gain so much popular following that the Republican administration succeeding Truman's would feel obliged to conciliate them not only by rhetoric but by a purge of the State Department China hands.

Democrats who came to office in the 1960s assumed that the venom of McCarthy and his like had contributed to their party's defeat in 1952 and 1956. The bureaucrats who advised them remembered no less well the consequences of Truman's China policy. Both groups were fearful of what might happen at home if another Democratic administration "lost" another part of Asia. In his memoirs Lyndon Johnson is quite explicit on the point.

Listing reasons for not having deserted South Vietnam, he puts first in order: "A devisive debate about 'who lost Vietnam' would be . . . even more destructive to our national life than the argument over China had been."[11]

3. *The tough-mindedness of the decision makers.* Truman enjoyed making decisions. Had his principal advisers united in recommending military intervention in China, he would probably have accepted that recommendation with fewer qualms than Kennedy and Johnson displayed about acting in Vietnam. In 1950 he was to show little or no hesitancy about going to war in Korea to counter what he interpreted as an attempt by Stalin to repeat the tactics of Hitler. Truman was equally capable, however, of a decision not to act. With advice to such effect from Marshall and Lovett and evidence that Congress would not rebel, he made this choice.

Similarly, Marshall and Lovett were men given to confronting issues and deciding them one way or the other. As a professional soldier, Marshall was accustomed to envisioning the worst contingencies that could occur. During the war, Marshall had frequently said no to otherwise attractive proposals because he judged that, if the worst happened, the costs would be excessive. As a banker, Lovett, too, had had experience in saying no and in rejecting investment opportunities that entailed a high risk of having to send good money after bad. In the summer and autumn of 1947, Marshall and Lovett may have been uncertain about military involvement in China. By the winter of 1947–48 they had concluded that the commitment would be of uncertain magnitude and indefinite duration. They decided that the commitment should not be made, accepting the consequent certainty that the Nationalists would eventually lose.

Kennedy, Johnson, and the majority of their advisers were not equally decisive. Neither president was prepared to face up to the worst that might happen in Vietnam and determine whether he would or would not pay the price to prevent it. With only a few exceptions, the same was true of the men who gave them counsel. Rusk never translated his doubts into a resolute recommendation against committing American prestige to the "losing horse." Until it was too late to be useful, McNamara did not press upon the president an argument that the rescue of South Vietnam would cost more than it was worth. Of course, a conception of possible consequences that included limited and sublimited war as well as all-out war made Kennedy, Johnson, and their advisers more adventurous, while memories of the domestic results of abandoning China made them more timid. Also, Marshall and Lovett had just fought a major war. They had no subconscious or conscious need to display *machismo*. Even so, one feels that there was an additional difference and that Truman, Marshall, Lovett, and perhaps also Vandenberg had a little more steel in their makeup.

Organizational Factors

Also important were factors which might be classified as structural:

4. *A relatively uncomplex executive branch.* While the reader may feel that he has travelled a maze of missions, divisions, offices, etc., he would feel

this much more keenly if the analysis had centered on Vietnam. For by the 1960s the National Security Council staff had become a bureaucracy unto itself, headed by assistants to the president who were sometimes more influential than cabinet officers. In the State Department, six to eight layers of undersecretaries, assistant secretaries, deputy assistant secretaries, and the like had grown up between the secretary and the desk officers who knew something about a place like Vietnam. The missions abroad were mini-governments with numerous specialized subunits. The office of the secretary of defense had expanded. Within it, an assistant secretary for International Security Affairs ran a little State Department, with a policy planning staff, regional divisions, and desk officers all his own. The Joint Chiefs of Staff had a much more elaborate structure. The services had not lagged in their own bureaucratic growth. And the Central Intelligence Agency not only housed thousands of specialized analysts but also maintained a vast network of overseas stations and facilities.

The fragmentation of the executive branch had created difficulties in 1945–49. Not only the embassy but also each of the advisory groups and military commands in China had made policy recommendations to Washington. Responses to their recommendations required reconciliation of views among various segments of the State Department and the armed services. Sometimes they produced interdivisional or interdepartmental battles. The varieties of opinion elicited, the varieties of personal vanity that became engaged, and the varieties of interests that had to be reconciled all made it immensely difficult for busy, preoccupied men such as Truman, Marshall, Lovett, and Forrestal to determine which decisions *had* to be made and what their costs would be.

Even so, Truman and his chief advisers were dealing with a small circle of men. In most cases, they knew them well enough to calibrate their judgments and discount for their private or parochial interests. Though making decisions under conditions of high uncertainty, they could feel that they understood most of the factors perceived as critical by the men who had more intimate knowledge of the specific problem.

In the executive branch of the 1960s, this condition may occasionally have obtained during a brief period of crisis, as, most notably, when the Soviets were discovered to have sited offensive missiles in Cuba. It probably did not exist for any long period of time with regard to any problem, and certainly not with regard to Vietnam. (At least until 1966, when, as it was said, Lyndon Johnson became the Vietnam desk officer.) As a result, the inevitable uncertainty surrounding any policy issue was magnified. The men with authority to make decisions were much less sure whom to trust or what to take into account. The gigantism of the executive branch thus joined with factors in the psychologies of men in power to promote avoidance of conclusive action.

5. *Simpler executive-legislative relations.* In view of the Senate Foreign Relations Committee's role as a critic of involvement in Vietnam and the legislation subsequently enacted to curb "the imperial presidency," one might

be tempted to conclude that an important difference was the relative power of Congress. In fact, this was not the case.

Congress itself did not lose authority between the late 1940s and 1960s. It was only the Foreign Relations Committee that did. In 1947—48 the decision of Vandenberg and his colleagues about intervention in China was conclusive. Not even the Appropriations committees could successfully challenge them, and an appeal on behalf of Chiang from members of the House Armed Services Committee had little more influence than if it had come from members of the Committee on Post Offices and Post Roads.

In the decade and a half that elapsed before the intervention in Vietnam, this condition changed. It was due partly to differences in personnel. J. William Fulbright of Arkansas, the Foreign Relations Committee chairman in the 1960s, was not like either Arthur Vandenberg or Tom Connally. He had more brains than either but less diplomacy, managerial skill, or capacity for influencing other legislators. Also, there were changes in Congress complementing changes in the executive branch. As aid programs became normal instruments of policy rather than new departures, appropriations became more important than authorizing legislation, and the Appropriations committees gained strength. As the military establishment increased in size and multiplied its activities abroad, the two Armed Services committees waxed in influence. The same was true of the select committee that oversaw the CIA.

In 1947—48 members of the Truman administration could look to the Foreign Affairs and Foreign Relations committees to voice the will of Congress. Once Marshall knew that the Foreign Relations Committee would support him rather than Forrestal or Wedemeyer, he knew that his decision and the president's had been confirmed. It was United States policy, and he could insist upon it. The same was to hold true in 1950, when Truman could consult informally with members of the Foreign Relations Committee and come away confident that Congress would not only support his intervening in Korea but approve of his doing so in compliance with a United Nations resolution and without a formal declaration of war.

In the 1960s, had Rusk been a resolute opponent of military intervention in Vietnam and had he secured the provisional backing of Kennedy and then the full support of the Foreign Relations Committee, he would not have been in the position of Marshall in the spring of 1948. Proponents of alternative Vietnam policies could still have obtained blessing from the Appropriations or Armed Services committees. If so, the majority of Congress would have been at least as likely to side with these other committees as with Senator Fulbright's. There was no longer a simple way in which the executive branch could ascertain the will of Congress.

In fact, none of the organs of Congress took exception to the intervention in Vietnam. The Foreign Relations Committee only began to do so after limited intervention escalated into large-scale warfare. The Appropriations and Armed Services committees registered little or no dissent until much later. Had members of one or another of these committees been asked whether preservation of a non-Communist Vietnam was no important an objective that it should be pursued even if hundreds of thousands of American troops had to be sent into combat, they might well have said yes. That is not the crucial point. Rather, it is that by the 1960s *no* committee had the authority to speak for Congress in answer to such a question. Along with the psychology of the policy makers and the complex structure of the executive branch, this fact, too, contributed to making decision more difficult than it had been earlier.

Environmental Factors

Finally, there were several factors which one might regard as environmental:

6. *Some Americans knew something about China.* This point needs little elaboration. Especially in the Office of Far Eastern Affairs, the State Department had functionaries who knew the Chinese language and had followed Chinese affairs continuously for two decades or more. They did not all agree: Vincent and Drumwright, for example, held quite different views. Debate between the two, however, was relatively sophisticated. In 1961—65, debate about Vietnam at a comparable level of government was much less well informed, more crude, and more abstract.

Moreover, some hundreds, perhaps even thousands, of private citizens knew as much or almost as much about China as did people inside the government. They were scholars, newspapermen, missionaries, businessmen, or the children of missionaries or businessmen who had resided in China. Like the China hands in government, these citizens held diverse opinions. With regard to the efficacy of American military intervention, the scholars and journalists tended to be as skeptical as Vincent, or even more so, and they made their opinions known. John K. Fairbank, the leading American historian of China, debated Judd and other interventionists on the popular radio forums, "Chicago Roundtable" and "Town Meeting of the Air." Theodore H. White and Annalee Jacoby published *Thunder out of China* (New York: Harper, 1946) a best seller and Book-of-the-Month club selection, which portrayed the Nationalists as corrupt reactionaries not worth rescuing.

Although the missionaries and children of missionaries were by no means united in support of Chiang, most of those who advocated intervention fell into this category. As with Judd and Luce, their experience of China was some years in the past. Although there is no evidence to such effect, this fact may have been noticed by policy makers. To be sure, a Gallup poll reported fifty-five percent of the public favoring aid to Chiang and only thirty-two percent opposing it; and Vandenberg assessed public opinion as "deeply sympathetic with China. . . . [and] her resistance against communism even more than Europe's against communism" (see Documents 5-h and 6-c). Even so, policy makers may have felt some concern lest articulate people like Fairbank and White criticize intervention and, because of their expertise, win a following.

In any case, the very possibility of a public challenge from outside experts forced decision makers to think about the rationales for intervention or nonintervention that would meet such a challenge. Because almost no private citizens knew anything about Vietnam, the decision makers of the early 1960s had less cause either to reckon on a public debate or to reason out the pros and cons as they might be perceived by people outside the government.

7. *Decisions were made by a well-settled administration with an election close at hand.* Truman was in his third year of office when the question of whether or not to intervene in China came to a head. He had passed through his transition period in 1945—46. Like his predecessors and successors, he had discovered from experience that bureaucrats usually had parochial perspectives and that their judgment of the "national interest" was no better than his own. He had developed ways of identifying real issues and learned whom to trust and not trust. Although Marshall and Lovett were new to their jobs, they were old Washington hands. They, too, understood how not to be hustled.

In 1947—48, furthermore, Truman had a presidential election immediately ahead of him. Though there is not a particle of supporting evidence, it can be surmised that he would have seen even limited military intervention in China as potentially harmful to his candidacy. It would add to the armory of issues available for Henry Wallace, who was to challenge him as the candidate of a left wing third party. Because of probable criticism from China experts in universities and among newspapermen, intervention might alienate anti-Communist and anti-Wallace liberals such as those who had recently formed Americans for Democratic Action. Worse still, it could produce some casualties or deaths, lead Republicans to revive charges that the Democrats were the war party, and disrupt bipartisan cooperation on aid to Europe and other such policies. Though Truman could expect criticism for not aiding Chiang, he could have calculated realistically and accurately that most of the attacks would come later, after Chiang fell. Except at the margin, they were not likely to affect the presidential vote in 1948. In fact, Gallup polls as late as December 1948 were to show the public still uncertain about what was happening in China and divided as to what the response of the United States should be (see Document 6-k).

Whether or not the president himself took account of the approaching election, some of his advisers must have done so. Marshall and Lovett cannot have been unconscious that the course of action which they recommended did not run counter to Truman's interests as a candidate. Probably sharing the almost universal opinion that Truman would not be reelected and that a Republican would take over the presidency in January 1949, they may also have seen it as both prudent and patriotic not to precommit the next administration to carrying on a war. Even in face of a Soviet attempt to take over Berlin, they were circumspect about adopting a course of action which a new administration would be unable to reverse.

A further effect of the impending election was to diminish the sense of urgency among those who advocated intervention. Members of the missions in China, officers of the military establishment, and men such as Judd and Bridges may have felt that an effort to get a change of policy by Truman was not worthwhile. Instead, they should wait and work on the new president.

In the early 1960s, both sets of conditions were different. Kennedy in 1961 and Johnson in 1963—65 were presidents still settling in. Neither had reached the stage of knowing when and when not to trust advice from the bureaucracy, and neither had yet arrived at a final estimate of the strengths and weaknesses of his appointed advisers. Especially in view of the more complex structure of the executive branch, they were more likely to be influenced by cables from Saigon than was Truman by 1947—48 to be influenced by cables from his emissaries in China. In 1961, Rusk, McNamara, and men like them were in the same situation as the president. In 1963—65 these men had some experience, but none knew whether he possessed the new president's confidence. Hence, even if so disposed, they might have felt reluctant to force upon him a choice between their advice and that of the diplomats and soldiers nearer the scene.

Moreover, Kennedy in 1961 was three years away from another presidential election. Especially because of the "loss of China" syndrome, the apparent incentives for him were different from those for Truman. If bad consequences followed from intervention in Vietnam, they could be faced in 1962 and 1963. The question of whether the price was too high could then be reviewed. On the other hand, if the United States did not intervene and the Communists took over South Vietnam, that fact would remain in evidence in 1964. Even if such thoughts did not enter Kennedy's mind, they may have crept into those of men around him.

Johnson in 1963 was heir to the commitment Kennedy had made. His best opportunity to make a real choice between rescuing or abandoning South Vietnam came almost immediately after his accession, when Diem was assassinated and one military coup after another occurred in Saigon. But Johnson could hardly confront such a choice at the very beginning of a transition period and with an election less than year away. What he did was to procrastinate. Until the election, he attempted neither to increase nor reduce the level of military involvement. Only after November did he face up to his options; and then, of course, he and his advisers were in a position like that of Kennedy in 1961.

8. *The Chinese were not the Vietnamese.* If only relying on American official reportage, one might regard Chiang and Diem as twins. Cables from China in 1945—49 and from South Vietnam in 1961—63 seem paraphrases of one another, characterizing either Chiang or Diem as leaders who had lost their dynamism and were losing their popular appeal; men who were unduly deferential to reactionary elements around them and unduly tolerant of corruption, especially by members of their own families; and men who would not institute reforms necessary to save their nations.

Probably, however, the chief likeness between Chiang and Diem was that Americans said the same things about them and the same things to them. Both leaders were beset by foreigners who nattered about reforms. Precisely what was wanted from them was seldom clear. For China, the most visionary summary was one put together in a working paper for the Wedemeyer mission. Compiled by Sprouse, it may have been deliberately overstated. In any case, it included abolition of the secret police; transfer of power from the national to local police forces; reduction and reorganization of the armed forces in order to make them efficient, professional, and nonpolitical; reduction in the number of government employees, discharge of those who were incompetent or corrupt or both, and formation of an honest and independent civil service; a fair and honestly administered system of taxation; freedom for the press; an end of government interference in universities; free elections in localities and provinces as well as in the nation as a whole; and some measures to bring about more even distribution of land and wealth.[12]

Although such programs were advocated as being in the interest of China and later of Vietnam, their proponents showed little or no comprehension of the specific needs of either Chiang or Diem. For, like almost all heads of Government, Chiang and Diem assumed that the paramount interest of the nation was their retention in office. To this end, it seemed crucial, for example, that there be some instrument of terror such as a secret police; that there not be efficient armies other than those whose loyalty was certain; that potential conspirators be bought off with jobs or bribes; that the press and universities not be able to foment subversion; and that powerful landowners be placated rather than turned into malcontents. Chiang and Diem had identical problems in that both wanted American aid and both had to deal with Americans whose conditions for extending aid were such as to threaten their own holds on power.

In other respects, resemblances between the two were less close. Though the Chinese and Vietnamese had the same cultural heritage, their histories in modern times had been very different. Chiang came from a line of Chinese rulers who had managed barbarians by playing one off against another. As his situation worsened in 1947—48, he resorted to the expedient of letting the Americans know that he contemplated turning to the Soviet Union for mediation and subsequent protection. He also tried to make them believe that, if they did not supply him with arms, the British would do so. He sought in various ways to get Americans into positions in which they would find themselves fighting the Communists. Despite some reports to the contrary by Stuart, it was only in late 1948, after his outlook became desperate and after Truman had been reelected, that Chiang began to suggest placing himself in the hands of Americans and giving American officers powers beyond those of foreign advisers employed by previous Chinese rulers.

Chiang's rivals were equally circumspect. Except for Marshal Li Chi-shen, who was in exile in Hong Kong and had no real base in China proper, none of them bid for American backing by promising outright to be more obedient to American bidding. At most, they attempted to persuade the Americans that their programs were more consistent with American ideals.

The Vietnamese, by contrast, were products of a colonial past. They were schooled in getting their way by manipulating foreigners whom they pretended to obey. For all his nationalistic rhetoric and independence of character, even Diem was prepared to make apparent concessions that Chiang would not make. And Vietnamese generals had little hesitation about trying to involve Americans in their plans for coups. It may well be that the principal reason why the United States did not intervene militarily in China, as it later did in Vietnam, was that the Chinese did not exert themselves as wholeheartedly and adroitly to bring about American intervention.

Determining the Decisive Factors: The Limits of Historical Analysis

This list of variables is not exhaustive. One can imagine, for example, that the Kennedy administration might have viewed Vietnam differently had it not experienced humiliation only six months earlier in landing Cuban exiles at the Bay of Pigs and having them routed by Fidel Castro's forces. One can also imagine that Truman and even Marshall and Lovett might have felt differently about China if Chiang had been overthrown and assassinated as Diem was to be in 1963, and they felt that the missions in China bore some responsibility for having brought a successor regime into power.

But the crucial variables were probably neither random events of this sort nor wholly nonrandom factors such as realities of power, long-term historical trends, or economic forces. Instead, they were certain persisting ideas in the minds of decision makers, certain elements in their characters, certain qualities in the governmental structure, and certain features in the domestic and international environment.

To be explicit, I feel that the eight factors listed above were decisive. Had all been present in 1961–65, the Kennedy and Johnson administrations would not have intervened militarily in Vietnam. On the other hand, had the conditions of 1961–65 obtained in 1945–49, the United States would have made some kind of military commitment in China. I am even inclined to think that if any one of these factors had been other than it was, the outcome might have been different.

It is hardest to argue such a case for the structural factors. Had the policy makers of 1945–49 been more removed from the presumed experts, and had they been exposed to wider varieties of bureaucratic pressures, they would have found it harder to decide that nonintervention was clearly the preferable policy; but they might still have decided as they did.

Had Truman and his advisers not been able to obtain a conclusive verdict from Congress, they would have had a more difficult time. Marshall would have had to expend as much effort on the Pentagon initiatives of 1948 and the Tsingtao question as on the China Aid Act. If so, he and the others might have relented. On the other hand, they might equally well have stood fast.

Conversely, the Kennedy and Johnson administrations might have gone into Vietnam as they did even if the executive branch had been less complex and if there had been a way of having Congress face up to the issue and participate in deciding it. The involvement of the congressional leadership had a good deal to do, to be sure, with the Eisenhower administration's decision not to intervene in support of the French in Vietnam in 1954. Even so, it is possible that Congress in the 1960s would have pressed the Kennedy and Johnson administrations to take military action rather than to refrain from doing so. Structural factors seem to me to have the least explanatory power.

Psychological factors probably made more difference. If Truman, Marshall, and Lovett had been accustomed to think in terms of limited wars or "brush-fire" wars, they might well have found it harder to resist the recommendations of Wedemeyer, Cooke, and the missions in China. Had they been men of less self-confidence, they would probably have looked more favorably on compromise formulae somehow testing the possibility of putting military advisers into China. They might have been tempted, for example, by the idea of attaching such advisers to Nationalist units south of the Yangtse. Had Marshall and Lovett had reason to foresee furore such as actually arose over the "loss" of China, they would surely have been more hesitant to advise the president as they did.

One can imagine without great difficulty that Vietnam decisions might have come out differently if members of the Kennedy and Johnson administrations had visualized war in terms of World War II rather than in terms of the Korean conflict or the counterinsurgency campaigns in Malaya and the Philippines; if Rusk had had the character and standing of Marshall (or perhaps even if Lovett had accepted Kennedy's offer and been secretary of state in place of Rusk); or if Kennedy, Johnson, and their advisers had been able to estimate public reaction to "losing" Vietnam without remembering what had followed the "loss" of China.

But most powerful of all in explaining the difference are the factors loosely classifiable as environmental. If Truman and his advisers had not had to expect a public debate about intervention in China, they would have been exposed only to the adversary process within the bureaucracy, and there the voices proposing action were stronger and more numerous than the voices on the opposing side.

If the Truman administration had been less experienced and less well settled, it would almost certainly have been more influenced by advice from Stuart, Wedemeyer, Cooke, and the Joint Chiefs. If Truman and Marshall had had to make their decision in 1949-50 instead of 1947-48, they might well have seen the arguments for military action as much more persuasive.

Almost certainly, Truman and his advisers would have seen the arguments differently even in 1947—48 if Chiang and other Nationalists had been steadily exerting themselves to persuade the American government to assume responsibility for their military success against the Communists.

It seems equally likely that Kennedy and Johnson would have had second thoughts if they had reckoned in advance on the amount and character of public debate which intervention in Vietnam would actually provoke; that they would have been more skeptical or cautious if they had had to make the critical decisions on Vietnam later in their presidencies; that this might have been true if presidential elections lay just ahead; and that these administrations would have regarded the issues quite differently if the Vietnamese had been as proud and independent and seemingly uncooperative as the Chinese Nationalists.

These observations are no more than musings. One cannot run the facts of political history through a computer and test whether the outcome would have been different if one variable was changed and the others remained constant. To ask why the United States government chose the option of nonintervention when confronted with the prospect of Communist conquest of China is nevertheless a useful exercise not only for achieving better understanding of the past but also for gaining better insight into issues that may arise in future.

Notes

1. U. S., Congress, Senate, Committees on Armed Services and Foreign Relations, Hearings on the Military Situation in the Far East, 82d Cong., 2d sess., 1951, p. 382.

2. *The Pentagon Papers*, Senator Gravel Edition, 4 vols. (Boston: Beacon Press, 1972), vol. 2, p. 105.

3. Ibid., pp. 108-9.

4. *FRUS*, vol. 7, 1947, p. 849.

5. Ibid., p. 849; *FRUS*, vol. 8, pp. 146-65.

6. *FRUS*, vol. 7, 1948, pp. 141-43.

7. See *FRUS*, vol. 7, 1945, pp. 1235-6; *FRUS*, vol. 7, 1947, pp. 1132-4.

8. *FRUS*, vol. 7, 1945, pp. 1210-1, 1246-7, 1361-2, 1388-9; *FRUS*, vol. 10, 1946, pp. 1230-2, 1238, 1240-4, 1374-7.

9. *FRUS*, vol. 7, 1945, pp. 1229-30; *FRUS*, vol. 10, 1946, pp. 1380-1; *FRUS*, vol. 7, 1947, pp. 1373-6.

10. This point was suggested to me by Albert O. Hirschman.

11. Lyndon B. Johnson, *The Vantage Point: Perspectives in the Presidency, 1963-69* (New York: Holt, Rinehart, and Winston, 1971), p. 152.

12. *FRUS*, vol. 7, 1947, pp. 726-30.

part two

Documents of the Decision

1

Wartime Policy and the Outlook from Washington After the War

Document 1-a†

United States Policy Objectives Defined: January, 1945

The short-term objective of the United States Government is to assist in mobilizing all of China's human and material resources for prosecution of the war against Japan. We are using our influence to bring about a great degree of political and military unity, and to achieve greater efficiency and volume in the production of war material. We are supplying China with materials for direct military use and for industrial purposes connected with the war effort.

Our long-term objective in China is to assist in the development of a united, democratically progressive, and cooperative China which will be capable of contributing to security and prosperity in the Far East. . . .

We would like to see the rearmament, to such extent as may be practicable, of all Chinese forces willing to fight the Japanese, but the present unsatisfactory relations between the Chinese Government and the Chinese Communists makes it impolitic to undertake measures for the rearmament of the Chinese Communists even though it is generally conceded that they could effectively use quantities of small arms ammunition and demolition materials. However, if operations are undertaken along the China coast it is suggested that our military authorities should be prepared to arm any Chinese forces which they believe can be effectively employed against the Japanese, and that they should at an opportune time so advise the Chinese military authorities.

It is our purpose, as indicated above, to utilize our influence to bring about, both as a short-term and as a long-term objective, the unification of China. It does not necessarily follow that China should be unified under Chiang Kai-shek. However, with regard to the short-term objective, Chiang appears to be the only leader who now offers a hope for unification. The alternative to the support of Chiang for the attainment of our immediate

---

†From: Memorandum by John Carter Vincent, chief of the Division of Chinese Affairs, January 29, 1945, in U. S., Department of State, *Foreign Relations of the United States*, vol. 7, 1945, pp. 37-38. (Hereafter referred to as *FRUS*.)

objective might be chaos. With regard to our long-term objective, it is our purpose to maintain a degree of flexibility which would permit cooperation with any leadership in China that would offer the greatest likelihood of fostering a united, democratic, and friendly China. Developments in this regard would of course have a bearing on any plans to assist in the peace-time rearmament of China.

Document 1-b†

"The Situation in China: A Discussion of United States Policy with Respect Thereto"

It will be clear that the situation in China has reached a critical state and that the developments of the next few weeks will have a momentous bearing on the future of China, of the Far East and of the world.

It is evident that the Chinese Communists are making a supreme effort to assert control of north China. It is becoming more and more clear that the Chinese Communists are, furthermore, making a strong bid to seize control of Manchuria. It appears that in this effort to absorb Manchuria, the Chinese Communists have been aided and abetted by the U.S.S.R. which has been in control of all or parts of Manchuria since about the middle of August 1945. Without Soviet assistance, it is difficult to see how the Chinese Communists could have become so securely entrenched in Manchuria as they appear to be today. . . .

It is assumed that our primary objective in this uncertain and disordered world—certainly prior to the establishment of an effective world organization to ensure world peace—is the promotion of the security of the United States.

What policy or policies should we follow with respect to China in order to attain this primary objective—the security of the United States? It has been our traditional policy to advocate and support respect for the territorial integrity and political independence of China. As a corollary to that policy we have sought the emergence of a strong, unified, progressive government in China. Since 1928 we, in common with the great majority of the Powers, have recognized the National Government of China as the legitimate government of China and have had continuous relations with it. Since the Japanese attack on Pearl Harbor we have been allied with that government in waging war against Japan. Indeed, one of the prime reasons for the Japanese decision to attack us lies in our defense of the National Government of China. . . .

How may we best safeguard our security and interests in the light of developments in China as described above?

We appear to be faced with two major alternatives: (1) to give vigorous and sustained support to the National Government to the end that it may

---

†From: Memorandum by Everett Drumwright, chief of the Division of Chinese Affairs, Department of State, November 16, 1945, in *FRUS*, vol. 7, 1943, pp. 629-34.

obtain effective control of all parts of China, including Manchuria; or (2) withdrawal of our support from the National Government and of our armed forces and facilities from China. . . .

It is submitted that, in the interests of our own security and peace and stability in the Far East, we should move resolutely and effectively to assist the National Government of China to effect restoration of the recovered areas of China, including Manchuria. We appear to be on firm legal and moral grounds in pursuing such a policy, and its implementation will, it seems clear, offer the best opportunity for the unification of China and diminution of the possibility of foreign intervention. Failure to afford substantial assistance to the National Government in this respect is likely to result in the creation in Manchuria and perhaps in parts of north China and Inner Mongolia of a strongly entrenched Chinese Communist regime contiguous to the U.S.S.R. . . . Such a Communist regime could hardly be expected to regard the United States in a friendly light. The United States, bearing in mind the close ideological and other ties that exist between the Chinese Communists and the U.S.S.R. could scarcely, for its part, view the development of such a state, de facto or otherwise, with equanimity. Considering the character, the ideology and the past attitude of the Chinese Communists, it is difficult to perceive how American interests of any kind could flourish in such a Communist state. The creation of such a Communist state would seem, in effect, to bring about a situation which in many important particulars would be little different from that obtaining before the defeat of Japan. Instead of a Japanese-dominated puppet regime we should probably find in its place one dominated by the U.S.S.R. Obviously such a development is neither one that was contemplated by us when we went to war with Japan nor one that will promote the security and interests of the United States. . . .

It is submitted that in the implementation of our policies towards China we should be guided primarily, as has been stated above, by considerations of our own security interests. Other considerations, such as democracy in China, questions as to the relative efficiency of the two contending factions, the question of "fratricidal strife", et cetera, would thus seem to be of secondary concern and should accordingly be so regarded at this time. . . .

It is submitted that any policy of American withdrawal from China at this juncture or of half-hearted assistance to China will destroy what we wish to achieve—a strong, united China with close and friendly attachments to the United States. It goes without saying that a disunited China or a China that is unfriendly towards the United States will be an ever-present menace to the security of our country and inimical to the principles which we espouse.

Document 1-c†

"A Desperate State of Affairs"

The cabinet luncheon started out by the President walking in with a roll of teletype yellow paper in his hand, saying, "See what a son-of-a-bitch did to me." Then he proceeded to read the story of Pat Hurley's resignation as it had been given out just a half hour previously. . . .

The subject then shifted over to the desperate state of affairs in China. . . . The President said that both England and Russia wanted a weak and divided China. He said we were the only big nation that wanted a united democratic China. The President said that unless we took a strong stand in China, Russia would take the place of Japan in the Far East. I thought to myself, "This (the President's attitude) means World War Number 3." Byrnes said that the Chinese Nationalists have informed the State Department that the Chinese communists now have lots of Russian tanks and guns. I couldn't help remembering that when I was in China in June of 1944 the Chinese Nationalists were continually claiming that the Russians, as the result of their pact with Japan, were pulling out their troops in a way to permit Japanese troops to fight against the Generalissimo. . . . It all sounded to me like the Chinese Nationalists were playing the game which I suspected them of when I was there in June of 1944, namely, "Doing their dammdest to provoke a war between the United States and Russia." With all our superiority in material things I am inclined to think that the Chinese are smarter than we are in the psychology of diplomacy.

Jimmie Byrnes outlines his policy as being one of using our armed forces to disarm the Japs in China and Manchuria. . . . At the conclusion of getting the Japs out Jimmie Byrnes thought the United States should stand pat and not give Chiang Kai-shek anything whatsoever until he agreed to come to terms with the Chinese communists and give them some places in a combination cabinet. Jimmie Byrnes again quoted what Stalin said to the President at Potsdam about the Chinese communists. It appears that Stalin called them brigands, robbers, and fascists. He also said that Stalin was for backing up the Generalissimo, thus furnishing the only hope for a strong central government in China. The various statements seemed to be as utterly contradictory as Hurley's own actions of the past month.

Jimmie Byrnes spoke at some little length about Bob La Follette, how exceedingly anti-Russian he was and how he believed that Russia was going to take over all of China. Bob La Follette advocated, according to Jimmie Byrnes, that the United States keep her troops more or less indefinitely in China until a stable government was really assured. It is amusing to see the way in which La Follette has now swung around to become an interventionist. Apparently those who had a large German constituency were

†From: Diary note on a cabinet meeting, November 27, 1945, in *The Price of Vision: The Diary of Henry A. Wallace, 1942-1946*, John M. Blum, ed. (Boston: Houghton Mifflin, 1973), pp. 519-522. Reprinted by permission of the Houghton Mifflin Company.

for a strong America First policy prior to 1942, whereas today the same people are strong interventionists and anxious to follow a policy which would eventually get us into a war with Russia.

Clinton Anderson urged that General Marshall be appointed at once as ambassador to take Hurley's place. The President said he planned to put General Marshall in as head of the Red Cross. This job would not be open, however, until March. When we left the cabinet luncheon the President and Jimmie Byrnes were getting ready to get hold of Marshall to talk him into going out to China. It was also suggested that he stop off in Moscow on the way. Marshall is very strongly anti-Russian and if he takes the job this may produce a rather unusual situation.

2

General Marshall's Mission to China

Document 2-a†

Directives for Marshall's Mission

The President stated that he wished to have a clear and complete understanding among us as to just what was the basis on which I' was to operate in China in representing him. Mr. Byrnes outlined the policy of this Government as he understood it and advocated it. In effect he stated this, that first of all we, that is the Army and Navy, were being authorized to proceed at once with the arrangement of shipping for the transfer of the armies of the Generalissimo to Manchuria and for their logistical support; also for the evacuation of Japanese from China; and finally, though this was to be maintained in a status of secrecy, for the present, for the transfer of the Generalissimo's troops into North China for the purpose, on our part, of releasing the Japanese forces in that area and facilitating their evacuation and deportation to Japan.

Mr. Byrnes stated that the reason for holding secret for the present the preparations for the movement of the Generalissimo's troops into North China was to enable General Marshall to utilize that uncertainty for the purpose of bringing influence to bear both on the Generalissimo and the Communist leaders towards concluding a successful negotiation for the termination of hostilities, and the development of a broad unified Chinese government.

The President stated his concurrence with the proposition outlined by Mr. Byrnes and informed General Marshall that he would back him in his, General Marshall's, efforts whatever they might be to bring about the desired result.

General Marshall stated that his understanding then was that he would do his best to influence the Generalissimo to make reasonable concessions in his negotiations with the democratic and communist leaders, holding in abeyance the information that this Government was actually preparing shipping to assist the Generalissimo in moving his troops into North China for the purpose of releasing the Japanese in that region and, incidentally, taking over

---

†From: Memorandum by General Marshall of a conversation with President Truman, Secretary of State Byrnes, and Admiral Leahy, December 11, 1945, in *FRUS*, vol. 7, 1945, pp. 767-69.

control of the railroads. That, on the other hand, he, General Marshall, was to utilize the same uncertainty as to the attitude of our Government toward the establishment of the Generalissimo's troops in North China in the effort to bring the Communist leaders to the point of making reasonable concessions in order to bring about desirable political unification. That in the event that the Communist leaders refused to make what, in General Marshall's opinion, were reasonable concessions, he was authorized to back the Generalissimo by assisting in the movement of troops into the region for the U. S. purpose of removing the Japanese.

Finally, General Marshall stated, that if the Generalissimo, in his (General Marshall's) opinion, failed to make reasonable concessions, and this resulted in the breakdown of the efforts to secure a political unification, and the U. S. abandoned continued support of the Generalissimo, there would follow the tragic consequences of a divided China and of a probable Russian reassumption of power in Manchuria, the combined effect of this resulting in the defeat or loss of the major purpose of our war in the Pacific. Under these circumstances, General Marshall inquired whether or not it was intended for him, in that unfortunate eventuality, to go ahead and assist the Generalissimo in the movement of troops into North China. This would mean that this Government would have to swallow its pride and much of its policy in doing so.

The President and Mr. Byrnes concurred in this view of the matter; that is, that we would have to back the Generalissimo to the extent of assisting him to move troops into North China in order that the evacuation of the Japanese might be completed.

There was some discussion and Mr. Byrnes re-stated the policy of this Government adding specifically that it was not the purpose of the U. S. to send additional troops, divisions—he mentioned, to China, that he was opposed to that and that it would be contrary to the expressions of policy he had made public up to this time. The President agreed with this point of view of the Secretary of State.

Document 2-b†

America's Commitment to Chiang Kai-shek: December, 1945

The President handed me a final draft of his letter of instructions together with the enclosures. . . .

I stated that my understanding of one phase of my directive was not in writing but I thought I had a clear understanding of his desires in the matter, which was that in the event that I was unable to secure the necessary action by the Generalissimo, which I thought reasonable and desirable, it would still be necessary for the U. S. Government, through me, to continue to back the

---

†From: Memorandum by General Marshall of a conversation with President Truman and Undersecretary of State Acheson, December 14, 1945, in *FRUS*, vol. 7, 1945, p. 770.

National Government of the Republic of China—through the Generalissimo within the terms of the announced policy of the U. S. Government.

The President stated that the foregoing was a correct summation of his direction regarding that possible development of the situation.

The Under Secretary of State, Mr. Acheson, confirmed this as his understanding of my directions.

Document 2-c†

General Marshall: Obstacles to Peaceful Unification

In this intricate and confused situation, I shall merely endeavor here to touch on some of the more important considerations—as they appeared to me—during my connection with the negotiations to bring about peace in China and a stable democratic form of government.

In the first place, the greatest obstacle to peace has been the complete, almost overwhelming suspicion with which the Chinese Communist Party and the Kuomintang regard each other.

On the one hand, the leaders of the Government are strongly opposed to a communistic form of government. On the other, the Communists frankly state that they are Marxists and intend to work toward establishing a communistic form of government in China, though first advancing through the medium of a democratic form of government of the American or British type. . . .

Sincere efforts to achieve settlement have been frustrated time and again by extremist elements of both sides. The agreements reached by the Political Consultative Conference a year ago were a liberal and forward-looking charter which then offered China a basis for peace and reconstruction. However, irreconcilable groups within the Kuomintang, interested in the preservation of their own feudal control of China, evidently had no real intention of implementing them. Though I speak as a soldier, I must here also deplore the dominating influence of the military. Their dominance accentuates the weakness of civil government in China. At the same time, in pondering the situation in China, one must have clearly in mind not the workings of small Communist groups or committees to which we are accustomed in America, but rather of millions of people and an army of more than a million men.

I have never been in a position to be certain of the development of attitudes in the innermost Chinese Communist circles. Most certainly, the course which the Chinese Communist Party has pursued in recent months indicated an unwillingness to make a fair compromise. It has been impossible even to get them to sit down at a conference table with Government representatives to discuss given issues. Now the Communists have broken off negotiations by their last offer which demanded the dissolution of the National Assembly and a return to the military positions of January 13th

---

†From: Statement by General Marshall, January 7, 1947, in U. S., Department of State, *The White Paper*, pp. 686-89.

which the Government could not be expected to accept.

Between this dominant reactionary group in the Government and the irreconcilable Communists who, I must state, did not so appear last February, lies the problem of how peace and well-being are to be brought to the long-suffering and presently inarticulate mass of the people of China. The reactionaries in the Government have evidently counted on substantial American support regardless of their actions. The Communists by their unwillingness to compromise in the national interest are evidently counting on an economic collapse to bring about the fall of the Government, accelerated by extensive guerrilla action against the long lines of rail communications—regardless of the cost in suffering to the Chinese people.

The salvation of the situation, as I see it, would be the assumption of leadership by the liberals in the Government and in the minority parties, a splendid group of men, but who as yet lack the political power to exercise a controlling influence. Successful action on their part under the leadership of Generalissimo Chiang Kai-shek would, I believe, lead to unity through good government. . . .

I have spoken very frankly because in no other way can I hope to bring the people of the United States to even a partial understanding of this complex problem. I have expressed all these views privately in the course of negotiations; they are well known, I think, to most of the individuals concerned. I express them now publicly, as it is my duty, to present my estimate of the situation and its possibilities to the American people who have a deep interest in the development of conditions in the Far East promising an enduring peace in the Pacific.

3

The Question of Military Aid to Nationalist China

Document 3-a†
Military Aid and American Interests

The "Military Advisory Group" paper provides for American personnel of approximately 1,000 Army officers and 2,600 enlisted men, and from 300 to 700 Navy personnel.

The Joint Chiefs of Staff recommend "promptness in initiating an orderly program of military assistance to the Chinese" because it "will tend to forestall them from seeking military assistance elsewhere". They say that "economic and political assistance (to China) should be carefully integrated at all times with the military assistance provided to China"! . . .

The Joint Chiefs of Staff list certain rights or concessions desired from China in return for our furnishing the Advisory Group. Important among these are: (1) complete exemption from any form of import duty or taxation on goods to be used or consumed by the personnel of the Group; (2) exemption from Chinese jurisdiction for all Group personnel, civilian as well as military; (3) China to refrain from supporting armed forces (Chinese) not sponsored by the U. S., when such support would interfere quantitatively or qualitatively with the effectiveness or efficiency of the U. S. sponsored units; (4) China may purchase military equipment from another power only after consultation with the Advisory Group; and (5) certain preferential treatment for American commercial organizations in China.

Comment:

The size and character of the Group, the statement of concessions desired, and the general tenor of the Joint Chiefs of Staff papers raise a question as to whether we are not moving toward establishment of a relationship with China which has some of the characteristics of a de facto protectorate with a semi-colonial Chinese army under our direction. . . .

---

†From: John Carter Vincent, director of the Office of Far Eastern Affairs, Department of State, to Secretary of State Byrnes, November 12, 1945, in *FRUS*, vol. 7, 1945, pp. 615-17.

We have stated on numerous occasions that we desire a free, unified, independent China with a government broadly representative of the Chinese people. It has also been made clear to China on many occasions that we do not intend that military assistance and advice shall be used in support of an administration not in conformity with the general policies of the United States, or in support of fratricidal warfare, or as a threat of aggression. We should have reasonable assurances that an Advisory Group of the size and character proposed would in fact encourage the development of a unified and democratic China. Chiang Kai-shek has in the past shown a decided preference for military methods, rather than political methods, in seeking a solution of internal difficulties in China and his methods have fallen short of success. It is not unreasonable to anticipate that American military assistance on the scale contemplated might encourage Chiang to continue along this line without promise of success, and discourage attempts at unity by peaceful methods. If an American Military Advisory Group could be effective in bringing into being a unified, democratic China and in the process not create international political difficulties with our Allies, there would be no question as to the advisability of setting up the Group. On the other hand if the Group serves simply to encourage Chiang to seek a settlement of his difficulties by means of force and if the maintenance of unity in China were to become dependent upon American military assistance in the form of materiel and advice, we would find ourselves in an unenviable, and perhaps untenable, position.

The President has indicated his approval "in principle" of a military mission for China and I believe that such a mission could serve a useful purpose but I also believe that its character, size, and probable activities, should be carefully and thoughtfully examined in the light of considerations set forth above. . . .

Finally, I may express my general conviction that interference in the internal affairs of China would not pay dividends and involvement in civil strife in China would occasion serious difficulties for us without compensatory advantages. I say this, not to discourage giving China military assistance and advice, but as a caution against what I detect as being certain concepts and features of the Group—its character, size, and relation to the Chinese Government—which may, unless restraint and judgment are used, have the effect of carrying the Group, and us, into the field of intervention and involvement in China's internal political and military affairs.

Certainly the Congress should be informed fully and in detail of the Group in advance of any negotiations the State Department undertakes with the Chinese Government looking toward the creation of the Group, because, upon the expiration of the President's emergency powers, Congressional authorization will be required to continue the Group in being.

Document 3-b†

View from the State Department: To Limit Military Involvement

My reaction . . . is that the size and contemplated activities of the Group are not in conformity with its "advisory" character. It would appear that, rather than establishing an Advisory Group on a military staff level, it is planned to send out a military training group which would permeate throughout the Chinese Army on an operational level. As a matter of comparison, the size of the Group—approximately 4,600 officers and men—is roughly equal to the British officer strength in the Indian Army under peace-time conditions. I recommend, therefore, that the plan be reviewed with a view to formation of an Advisory Group which would function only on military staff level and which would be greatly reduced in size. I should say that a personnel of not more than several hundred would be fully adequate to the task.

It is my belief that the immunities, privileges, and concessions which the Chinese Government is expected to grant in connection with the establishment of the Group are excessive. . . . I do not consider it wise to ask for a preferential position for the Group so extensive in character and I consider it ill-advised to make establishment of the Group conditional upon the grant by China of concessions in unrelated fields.

Finally, I would suggest that the paper be referred back to the Joint Chiefs of Staff with a view to obtaining closer and more detailed study of the relationship of the Group to the maintenance of our own and world security. The present plan might be construed as a projection of U. S. military power onto the Asiatic continent rather than as simply aid to China in modernizing its Army. I question whether, international relations and other matters considered, the program outlined . . . would actually contribute towards our security and world peace or towards political unity, and peace and prosperity in China.

Document 3-c‡

Establishing the Advisory Groups

The Secretaries of War and the Navy are authorized and directed to establish jointly a U. S. Military Advisory Group to China. The strength of the Advisory Group shall not exceed one thousand officers and men except as authorized by me in the light of possible future political and military developments.

---

†From: Secretary of State Byrnes to the State-War Coordinating Committee, January 5, 1945, in *FRUS*, vol. 10, 1946, pp. 810-11.

‡From: Truman to the secretaries of the State, War, and Navy departments, February 25, 1946, in *The White Paper*, pp. 339-40.

The Secretary of State will conduct the necessary negotiations with the Chinese Government.

The object of this Advisory Group will be to assist and advise the Chinese Government in the development of modern armed forces for the fulfillment of those obligations which may devolve upon China under her international agreements, including the United Nations Organization, for the establishment of adequate control over liberated areas in China, including Manchuria, and Formosa, and for the maintenance of internal peace and security.

Document 3-d†

Suggested Concessions from Chiang

I have the honor to offer a few suggestions as to possible American aid to the present Government of China when or if conditions within this country seem to make this advisable. It is assumed that there must be at least two prerequisites. One is that the Government cease all aggressive military operations against the Communist Party and the other that it be sufficiently reorganized to encourage the hope of drastic reforms and of progress toward the establishment of genuinely democratic institutions.

The Civil War took a new turn when the Communist Party toward the end of last year insisted on their two impracticable conditions and began military and other attacks in the expectation that the Government would within a few months be so weakened that they could then resume the peace talks on terms more favorable to themselves. Up to that time they gave real indications of wanting the fighting to cease, but since then they have repeatedly taken the offensive. This, with the rapidly worsening financial and economic situation, compelled the Government either to succumb or to avert the threatened collapse by strong measures. . . .

At this writing Government reorganization is still undecided. . . . Whatever the final outcome, President Chiang will emerge as more than ever the predominant figure. Through all of the incessant bickering and bargaining, the personal and partisan jealousies or ambitions, he has been himself unassailed while maneuvering to achieve a workable solution. It is, in my opinion, not so much that he is or strives to be a dictator in the accepted sense as that he is the only personality whom the others all respect and around whom they can rally. It still remains true that whatever policy he really wants can be put into effect and that therefore by winning his approval for constructive reforms these can most effectively be carried out. There is no other person or group who could be counted on to maintain the solidarity of the Kuomintang or to integrate this with minority parties. With all of his shortcomings he sincerely seeks the welfare of his country according to democratic principles. In accomplishing this he desires the utmost cooperation with the United States. There may be developments before long which will justify substantial aid to

†From: Ambassador Stuart to Secretary of State Marshall, March 26, 1947, in *FRUS*, vol. 7, 1947, pp. 84-86.

the Chinese Government. It may be worthwhile, therefore, to be considering in advance some of the forms which this might take.

Military Reorganization. Every other problem in China touches sooner or later on this one.... But to carry out such a reorganization American training personnel would be essential. This would also be the surest protection to the Communist Party whose troops should be absorbed into the National Army. The American Army Advisory Group program is comprehensive and no doubt admirably planned but unless there can be political stability in the near future the fine start already made will be wasted. With this strengthened, however, by American-directed army reorganization, the training of future officers ought to contribute largely to peace within China and elsewhere....

If within the next few months there is conclusive evidence of progressive reforms in the Government, and of the futility of further Communist armed resistance, it is conceivable that the Chinese Government might with the concurrence of ours make a proposal to the Communist Party leaders that they cease what can be merely disruptive guerilla activities and either join the new coalition government until the inauguration of the Constitution next December or become at once a recognized political party with full rights and protection. Certain areas might be temporarily reserved for their local administration pending the establishment of real popular suffrage. The American control of military reorganization should be an ample guarantee. If they refuse such an offer—whatever the real or declared reasons—their armed forces and all those discovered in acts of sabotage might be treated as disturbers of peace and order and obstructors of economic recovery. Any such undertaking should be accompanied by a standing invitation to all Communist Party members and fighting units to retract their former allegiance together with full publicity explaining the motives and appealing to all public-spirited citizens to give their loyal support.

Document 3-e†

The Joint Chiefs of Staff Advocate Military Aid

1. A study of the military aspects of United States policy toward China indicates that, however other factors in the general situation differ from those found elsewhere in the world where the United States and Soviet policies are in conflict, many of the security factors involved are very similar. In China, as in Europe and in the Middle and Far East, it is clearly Soviet policy to expand control and influence wherever possible. This policy is evidenced by Soviet pressure on those nations lying around the periphery of the Soviet sphere, whenever and wherever conditions are propitious. In the light of this policy, the objectives in China are in most respects similar to those found elsewhere. The principal difference between the situation in China and that in the Near

†From: The Joint Chiefs of Staff to the State-War-Navy Coordinating Committee, June 9, 1947, in *FRUS*, vol. 7, 1947, pp. 838-44.

and Middle East is that in China there does not exist a united national government on which effective resistance to Soviet expansionist policy may be based.

2. The Soviet program in China is obviously a long-range one. One apparent objective of this program, as indicated by current communist propaganda, and publicly affirmed by Stalin that "the quickest withdrawal of American forces in China is vitally necessary for the future peace," (from a release by Tass—Telegraphic Agency of the Soviet Union—dated 24 September 1946) is to exclude United States influence in China and replace it with that of Moscow. It is believed, however, that the vastness of China, coupled with other conditions which are peculiar to China, such as lack of organization, transportation and communications, have dictated a plan of progressive expansion with the immediate objective limited to the control of the great resources and industrial potential of Manchuria. Except for Manchuria, however, the Soviets probably would be satisfied if internal chaos in the remainder of China were continued. Such chaos in China would serve the interests of the USSR in at least two important respects. It would not only prevent any effective National Government resistance to realization of their aims in Manchuria but it would also facilitate their adoption of a next step into North China or Sinkiang, or both, after they have established and consolidated their control over Manchuria.

3. There is evidence that current Soviet intentions are to remove Manchuria from the Chinese economy and integrate it into the economy of Eastern Siberia. . . .

4. If the Soviets succeed in their efforts to integrate Manchuria into the Siberian economy, they will have gone far toward bringing about the economic and military self-sufficiency of the Soviet Far Eastern Provinces which has long been an important Soviet objective. Their control of the most important economic areas, coupled with a prolongation of internal strife in China, is likely to result in complete economic collapse of the National Government, or in its ultimate submission to Soviet and Chinese communist pressure. In either case, conditions would be such as to facilitate the eventual continued expansion of Soviet power in Asia southward through China and towards Indo-China, Malaysia and India. It is believed that the economic reconstruction of China is essential to her achieving political stability, for, without economic stability, the revolutionary factors underlying the current civil war cannot be eliminated.

5. Communists in China are frequently described as differing basically from communists found in other parts of the world. While they have not always followed the normal pattern of communist operations employed in other countries, it is believed that Chinese communists have merely adjusted their techniques and operations to fit the conditions found in agrarian and undeveloped China and to facilitate progress toward achievement of their long-range objectives in the Far East. That they have in some respects improved conditions in areas brought under their control is believed due not so much to deviations from normal communistic doctrine as to the appalling

conditions which existed in those areas prior to their gaining control. That improvement may, however, well prove to be temporary if the communists gain complete control of the Chinese Government. Without United States aid, these conditions are likely to continue and will offer fertile fields to further the spread of communism. It is believed, however, that the Chinese communists, as all others, are Moscow inspired and thus motivated by the same basic totalitarian and anti-democratic policies as are the communist parties in other countries of the world. Accordingly, they should be regarded as tools of Soviet policy. . . .

6. A factor of major importance, with regard to peace and security interests both of the United States and the world, is the position which China occupies in the United Nations. Due principally to United States support and insistence, China is considered as one of the great powers and, as such, shares with U. S., U. K., USSR and France a predominant responsibility for the maintenance of international peace and security. . . . As one of the great powers, China is also one of the permanent members of the Security Council and thus possesses the power of veto. A continuation of the Chinese civil war, to the point where the strength of the Chinese National Government would deteriorate and be overthrown by the communist forces, would have the effect of removing from the Security Council a Chinese government friendly to the United States and replacing it with one under the control of the USSR. . . .

7. It is believed that several courses of action are open to the United States with regard to China. On one hand, the United States can give assistance and strengthen the Chinese Government to the extent necessary to prevent Soviet expansion. Such a course of action would allow time for proper political action to be applied by the Chinese National Government and to take effect. On the other hand, the United States can choose to withdraw entirely from China and permit conditions in that country to drift further into chaos and disunity with the probable result that the Soviets will gain complete control over Manchuria and will sweep over the remainder of China. If this should occur, the United States must be prepared to accept eventual Soviet hegemony over Asia.

8. It is the understanding of the Joint Chiefs of Staff that the fundamental objective of United States policy toward China is to expedite the establishment of a stable representative government over a strong and unified China friendly to the United States. Soviet expansionist aims in China, furthered by the operations of Chinese communists, are clearly incompatible with this United States objective. In China, as elsewhere, it would appear that the threat of Soviet expansion will only be finally averted when, as a result of political development the Western concept of democracy and rights of the individual has proven to the Chinese its practical and ideological superiority over communism and other forms of totalitarianism. The nature and timing of this political action are matters beyond the competence of the Joint Chiefs of Staff. It is the opinion of the Joint Chiefs of Staff, however, that the military security of the United States will be

threatened if there is any further spread of Soviet influence and power in the Far East. Early countermeasures are called for if this danger of Soviet expansion is to be halted. With a disarmed and occupied Japan, the only Asiatic government at present capable of even a show of resistance to Soviet expansion in Asia is the Chinese National Government.

9. It is recognized that serious and difficult practical problems are involved in giving aid to the present Chinese National Government. Much American money and material assistance have been given and absorbed by China since the end of the war without any noticeable effect on the steadily worsening internal affairs of that country. China is so vast, the need of her people so great, and the politico-military situation so complex, that there may be some doubt as to whether any conceivable outlay of United States money and resources could be effective. It should be recognized, however, that the assistance which the United States has provided China since the end of the war has been piecemeal and uncoordinated. There have been no firm objectives based on a definite United States policy toward China other than the aspiration to influence the two major political elements to achieve a peaceful solution to their irreconcilable differences. Regardless of the corruption and the political shortcomings of the present National Government, it is believed that recent events have proven conclusively that under present circumstances the Chinese communists will only accept a solution which would assure their early control of the government and ultimate communist domination of China, which would jeopardize the military security of the United States.

10. The military problem in China involves important political, psychological and morale factors. A strengthened military posture on the part of the Chinese National Government may be of more importance, as the result of morale factors involved, in bringing about military success in their operations against the communists than will the operational use of any material assistance which we may contribute to the attainment of this posture. The Joint Chiefs of Staff do not have authoritative information on the specific needs of the Chinese National Government in the form of military equipment, assurance and advice, nor what material and economic aid and advice will be required to develop the sound economy necessary to build and maintain a strong military posture and unification of the country. This will require a detailed military and economic study. It is believed, however, that the latent resources and manpower of China are such that even small amounts of United States assistance to the National Government will materially strengthen its morale and at the same time weaken the morale of the Chinese communists. In this connection, the Joint Chiefs of Staff note that the President's 12 March 1947 message to Congress had this effect on the morale of the opposing elements of the Greek populace torn by dissidence strikingly similar to that in China. It is conceivable that the announcement of firm United States support of the National Government might cause the Chinese communists to accept the terms which have been offered them by the National Government in order to bring about cessation of hostilities. If

the Chinese communists do not accept these terms, it would appear that a relatively small amount of military assistance, in large part merely ammunition and replacement parts for American equipment furnished the National Government forces during and immediately following the recent war, should enable the National Government to establish control over areas now under Communist control.

11. In the light of the foregoing discussion it is the opinion of the Joint Chiefs of Staff that, from the military point of view, carefully planned, selective and well-supervised assistance to the National Government, under conditions which will assure that that assistance will not be misused, will definitely contribute to United States security interests. Such assistance should facilitate the military development which appears essential for the unification and stabilization of China. It should enable China more effectively to resist Soviet expansionist efforts in the Far East and will thus contribute to the military security of the United States. In addition, it should be a stabilizing factor throughout the Far East. A firm United States position in this regard, as in the Middle East and elsewhere in the world, would serve the cause of peace as well as the other aims of the United Nations.

Document 3-f†

Policy Differences Between the State Department and the Joint Chiefs of Staff

The fundamental difference in viewpoint between our Far Eastern Office and the JCS . . . lies in the answer each would give to the following questions: Is it good and feasible American policy to give direct and substantial military assistance to Chiang Kai-shek in his attempt to eliminate Communism from China by force?

The answer of the Far Eastern Office has been and is "no" because such a course (1) would lead inevitably to direct intervention in China's civil war; (2) would provoke the USSR to similar intervention on the side of the Chinese Communists; (3) would be inconclusive unless we were prepared to take over direction of Chinese military operations and administration and remain in China for an indefinite period; (4) would invite formidable opposition among the Chinese people; and (5) would constitute a strategic commitment in China inconsistent with . . . [a JCS study of May 10, 1947], which examines the problem of United States assistance to other countries from the standpoint of "urgency of need and importance to the national security of the United States" and places "China very low on the list of countries which should be given such assistance".

The JCS answer would seem to be "yes" (1) because Chiang can be assured of success in his campaign against the Communists by American military and economic assistance and (2) because failure to assist Chiang would result in

†From: Director Vincent to Secretary of State Marshall, June 20, 1947, in *FRUS*, vol. 7, 1947, p. 849.

USSR domination in China. With regard to the second point, in consideration of the administrative inefficiencies of the Chinese themselves, the magnitude of the task of dominating China, the easily aroused Chinese resentment at foreign interference, the lack of industrial development and material resources, and the inability of the Russians to give the material assistance necessary to make China a going concern, it is the opinion of the Far Eastern Office that a USSR-dominated China is not a danger of sufficient immediacy or probability to warrant committing ourselves to the far-reaching consequences which would ensue from our involvement in the Chinese civil war on the side of the National Government.

Document 3-g†

Marshall Seeks a Solution

For some time I have been considering what action we should take with relation to the rapidly deteriorating situation in China. The Joint Chiefs of Staff, and the War and Navy Departments I believe, are strongly in favor of supporting the Chinese Government both in a military way and in relation to the economy of the country. I felt as did Vincent that the Chiefs of Staff paper was not quite realistic and solutions were offered which were somewhat impracticable, particularly as to implementation in China. Nevertheless, the situation is critical and it is urgently necessary I feel that we reconsider our policy to see what changes may be necessary if any, regarding our continuing action in regard to China.

For about two weeks I have had in mind the probable desirability of sending Wedemeyer to China with a few assistants to make a survey of the situation and to report back at as early a date as possible. He is generally familiar with the China state of affairs and particularly with the important officials, and he is greatly esteemed by the Generalissimo. It so happened that during the past three days his name has been proposed to me by three different people outside of the Department representing the importance of doing something to clarify our situation with regard to China. I therefore brought Wedemeyer in quietly yesterday and discussed the situation with him, told him to think it over and come in today and give me his reactions. . . .

Up to the present moment I have kept this matter of Wedemeyer entirely to myself and I think until I get your reaction it should be confined to the two of us. If you and I reach an agreement then I think it would be necessary to bring Vincent into the matter, but not until then.

Please look this over and let me have your reaction tomorrow. It need not be in writing.

†From: Secretary of State Marshall to Under Secretary of State Lovett, July 2, 1947, in *FRUS*, vol. 7, 1947, pp. 635-36.

4

General Wedemeyer's Mission to China

Document 4-a†

Truman's Directive to Wedemeyer

You will proceed to China without delay for the purpose of making an appraisal of the political, economic, psychological and military situations—current and projected. In the course of your survey you will maintain liaison with American diplomatic and military officials in the area. In your discussions with Chinese officials and leaders in positions of responsibility you will make it clear that you are on a fact-finding mission and that the United States Government can consider assistance in a program of rehabilitation only if the Chinese Government presents satisfactory evidence of effective measures looking towards Chinese recovery and provided further that any aid which may be made available shall be subject to the supervision of representatives of the United States Government.

In making your appraisal it is desired that you proceed with detachment from any feeling of prior obligation to support or to further official Chinese programs which do not conform to sound American policy with regard to China. In presenting the findings of your mission you should endeavor to state as concisely as possible your estimate of the character, extent, and probable consequences of assistance which you may recommend, and the probable consequences in the event that assistance is not given.

Document 4-b‡

Wedemeyer's Recommendations

1. I have already indicated that I want to recommend moral encouragement and material aid.

2. The form, priority and extent of that material assistance to be determined by conferences between appropriate agencies of the two governments.

---

†From: President Truman to General Wedemeyer, July 9, 1947, in *FRUS*, vol. 7, 1947, pp. 640-41.

‡From: Memorandum by General Wedemeyer, September 7, 1947, in *FRUS*, vol. 7, 1947, pp. 769-70.

3. Such material assistance will be supervised to insure that it is not misdirected and is used fully in consonance with the policies of our government.

4. The supervisors or advisors should constitute a China Mission similar to that which we sent to Greece. The Mission to have a civilian head—preferably an outstanding economist who is dynamic, fearless, intelligent and experienced. The Mission Head should have authority to communicate direct to the State Department and other pertinent agencies of our government. However, the Ambassador would remain the diplomatic representative of the U. S. and would be responsible within the purview of his office for representations of high level government nature.

5. I feel that we should approach the Manchurian problem very much as we have already approached the Korean problem that is, that we attempt to establish a guardianship under five powers (U. S., USSR, Great Britain, France and China[)]. Failing this arrangement, for I believe Russia will refuse, then the matter should be referred to the United Nations for the establishment of a trusteeship. The request for guardianship and subsequently for trusteeship should be initiated by the Chinese Government. However, the United States could unquestionably make the suggestion that this course of action be taken.

5

Limited Military Aid to Nationalist China

Document 5-a†

Viewpoint of the Army Advisory Group: A Need for Emergency Measures

The present critical military and economic situation in China convinces me that now is the time for re-assessment not only of the scope and character of the activities of the Advisory Group, but also of the policy restrictions which limit our effectiveness. . . . Without the removal of these restrictions, further effort on our part can hope to achieve only rapidly diminishing results. Aside from these considerations, the tendency toward collapse of the present regime which is inherent in the existing military and economic crisis, if allowed to continue, may leave this Group in a position of complete, and possibly ridiculous, frustration. . . .

Consideration must therefore be given to some form of emergency assistance to China, and to an intensification of the training program, with the view of checking further deterioration of the military situation and of providing a firm basis for eventually restoring a satisfactory measure of stability. Such emergency assistance should take the form of equipment for training; of ammunition for training and for combat operations; of repair parts for weapons, for vehicles and for aircraft; and of additional transport aircraft to support combat operations. Lest these materials and supplies be ineffectively dissipated as has so often happened in the past, it would be essential that some form of control be established by agreement, as to their disposition and use. Should the exercise of this control be delegated to this Group, together with authority to regulate the flow of these supplies into China, it is felt that sufficient influence can be exerted to improve the strategy of operations and the quality of leadership. This, of course, presupposes that we would be permitted access to operational information in the field, and would be authorized to offer advice on operational matters to the Chinese. . . .

These emergency measures are suggested under the presumption that United States' interests in Manchuria are sufficiently vital to warrant such

---

†From: General Lucas, chief of the Army Advisory Group in China, to Ambassador Stuart, June 28, 1947, in *FRUS*, vol. 7, 1947, pp. 861-62.

overt action. If they are taken without delay, it is believed that there is a reasonable chance of maintaining a foothold in that area.

Document 5-b†

The Cost of Military Aid

The present unstable situation in China, viewed in the light of US-USSR tensions throughout the world, constitutes a source of international friction and is therefore a potential danger to the security interest of the US. A reasonably unified, non-Communist China, on the other hand, would probably serve to further American security interests; the emergence of such a state, moreover, would be damaging to the prestige of the USSR throughout the world.

It may be assumed that a Communist China would be closely aligned, politically, economically, and militarily, with the USSR. This situation would give the Soviet Union assured access to the food and raw material resources of North China and Manchuria and to naval and air bases in China; Chinese manpower reserves would probably be of only minor significance to the USSR. The development of a Chinese Communist state would tend to enhance the power of the Communist political movement in Asia and thereby contribute to the extension of Soviet influence in the world. If these prospective gains were to be exploited in full, however, the USSR would find it necessary to allocate from its scarce domestic resources capital equipment and possibly consumers' goods for the rehabilitation and development of the Chinese economy.

The probable cost to the US of securing China proper (excluding Manchuria) for the National Government can be estimated only within wide ranges. On the assumption that a minimum of internal economic stability is needed to maintain the National Government's military-political position, it is estimated that American non-military grants or credits totaling roughly US $2 billion would be required for the three-year period 1948-50. In order to have reasonable assurance of a Nationalist military victory over the Communists in China proper within the three years, it would be necessary for the US to provide military support in the form of equipment and continuing weapon and ammunition supplies for thirty Nationalist divisions. If the problem is viewed as one of restoring to Nationalist control all of China proper plus the Manchurian provinces, these estimates must be increased, perhaps by as much as 100 percent.

†From: Report by the Office of Intelligence Research, Department of State, September 18, 1947, in *FRUS*, vol. 7, 1947, pp. 286-87.

Document 5-c†

Rendering Effective Assistance: Increase Military Aid

The assistance presently given by the Army Advisory Group in China is greatly restricted due to the lack of instructions clearly outlining the scope of such assistance. As I interpret the purpose of the Military Advisory Group in China, we Americans are striving to assist them in overcoming the critical economic and military situation existing there. It is recognized that these conditions are the natural aftermath of eight years of war and that these conditions have been greatly confounded by the penetration and infiltration of Communism.

There have been so many delays and restrictions with reference to such assistance the past several months, actually conditions have deteriorated to an alarming degree. If the Military Advisory Group is to be continued in China and if it is to be of real assistance as above suggested, a clarifying directive should be dispatched at once to that group, removing current restrictions with reference to the scope of its activities. My recent observation in China caused me to recommend that the Military Advisory Group be permitted to assist the Chinese as suggested by the memorandum submitted to the American Ambassador on June 28, 1947 by Major General John P. Lucas [see Document 5-a]. The one restriction that I would include in any directive to Americans in the government service in China would be designed to preclude direct involvement in fratricidal warfare. It must be accepted that by indirection even today Americans are assisting the Nationalists in their struggle against the Chinese Communists, but I would not permit American military personnel in the operational areas of the current military conflict.

If our assistance to the National Government is to be timely and effective, the above ideas with reference to the Military Advisory Group should be implemented immediately. . . .

Document 5-d‡

Determining the Form of Assistance

Secretary Forrestal recalled that at the last meeting discussion on the Wedemeyer report had been deferred. He inquired what action the State Department was taking with respect to the report.

Secretary Marshall said that the State Department was actively working on the report and that particular attention was being given to the military phase as well as the financial phase. He said that the Department was studying the extent and the form of further assistance to the Chinese, and what controls would be necessary. He summarized by saying that apparently everyone is in

†From: Memorandum by General Wedemeyer, October 13, 1947, in *FRUS*, vol. 7, 1947, p. 893.

‡From: Minutes of a meeting with Secretary of State Marshall, Secretary of Defense Forrestal, and others, November 3, 1947, in *FRUS*, vol. 7, 1947, p. 911.

agreement that we wish to prevent Soviet domination of China and that we wish to do something to provide for a stable government there, but there is no unanimity on the way in which assistance can be rendered. He said that the immediate problem is to determine what can we do effectively. He said that we must recognize that we have the problem of prolonging the agonies of a corrupt government, and that we probably have reached the point where we will have to accept the fact that this government will have to be retained in spite of our desire to change its character. . . .

Document 5-e†

Rejecting Responsibility for Chinese Strategy and Plans

I am willing that Gen. Barr should make his advice available to Generalissimo on informal and confidential basis and that [Army Advisory Group] should supply advice with respect to reorganization of Chinese Army Services of Supply should that be desired. I am however not willing that we should accept responsibility for Chinese strategic plans and operations. I think you will agree that implications of our accepting that responsibility would be very far-reaching and grave and that such responsibility is in logic inseparable from authority to make it effective. Whatever the Generalissimo may feel moved to say with respect to his willingness to delegate necessary powers to Americans, I know from my own experience that advice is always listened to very politely but not infrequently ignored when deemed unpalatable.

Document 5-f‡

"Gambler's Choice in China"—An Opinion from the Left

To face the future in China requires of America a certain amount of courage. No likely solution will please our ethics or tradition. All we can seek is the solution that will be the least dangerous and costly.

Two ruthless groups are contending for the control of the people of China. Chiang rests on terror and American support; his terror is tempered by no return of more rice, more land or better living to the people. The Communists who contend with Chiang are ruthless men, too. But in return for the sacrifices they demand of the people, they give control of the land to the people who till it.

The policy advocated by those who demand support for Chiang is based upon these assumptions: that no matter how embarrassing Chiang's political countenance, he is good because he hates Communists; that communism everywhere is the same brutal conspiracy; that, finally, all Communists everywhere are tools of Moscow.

†From: Secretary of State Marshall to Ambassador Stuart, November 28, 1947, in *FRUS*, vol. 7, 1947, p. 923.

‡From: *The New Republic*, July 21, 1947, pp. 14-15.

All of these assumptions need careful study. Chiang, to be sure, hates Communists—but that in itself does not make him good. Hitler, too, hated Communists.

Communism, to be sure, has brutality sealed in the core of it; but in China, Chiang Kai-shek is far more brutal.

The last assumption—that all Communists are tools of Moscow—is the most dangerous. Beyond doubt the Chinese Communists are a Communist Party of the classic Marxist model. But they have a history of bitter disagreement with Moscow. The Chinese Communist Party has been riven again and again by the struggle between doctrinaire followers of the Kremlin and men who give their first allegiance to China herself. In China, the present leadership of the party is in the hands of native Chinese, not Moscow functionaries. When the Kremlin presses too closely, Chinese Communists rebel. Mao Tse-tung has in the past gone so far as to imprison Comintern representatives and to force their Chinese adherents out of his policy committee.

Nothing we can do will create democracy in China. A policy of nickel-and-dime aid cannot salvage Chiang from defeat—it must eventually force the Chinese Communists to seek aid in Moscow and commit their entire policy to Moscow's direction. . . .

The only policy left is one of complete withdrawal, a hands-off gamble. This gamble can mean that China relapses into unending strife and chaos, proving to the world that China as yet lacks the makings of greatness. Or, it can mean that the Chinese people will choose their own leadership and that this leadership will be responsible to Chinese interests alone, not to the military security of either the United States or the Soviet Union. This is an uncertain gamble; but these are the best alternatives that history can give us in this age of struggle.

Document 5-g†

"China: A Report to the American People"—An Opinion from the Right

To prevent the domination of China by any nation which might eventually mobilize the 450,000,000 Chinese for war against us is a vital interest of the United States.

Today Soviet Imperialism, using the Chinese Communists as instruments of its power politics, is striving to make China a Soviet satellite. In self-defense, therefore, we must keep China out of the hands of Stalin. But by what means? . . .

The problem must be attacked at once on three fronts: (1) economic and financial; (2) military; (3) political. Since the essence of the problem is the

†From: William C. Bullitt, "China: A Report to the American People," in *Life*, October 13, 1947, pp. 35 *et seq.*, and *The Reader's Digest*, December 1947, pp. 119-24. Copyright © 1947, Time Inc. Reprinted with permission of the publisher.

ejection of every armed Communist from China an intelligent project can be based only on an estimate of the time it will take to win the war. American military experts believe that this may take three years. Let us try to sketch a Three-Year Plan and estimate its cost.

1. During the next three years China will need large quantities of American cotton, tobacco, wheat, oil, gasoline, and many manufactured articles, from locomotives to spare parts for trucks. She will, therefore, need credits. The highest figure for such necessary credits given by American and Chinese economic experts is $250,000,000 a year—a tiny fraction of Europe's requirements. Let us scale that down to $200,000,000, and budget for our total Three-Year Plan $600,000,000 of credits for purchases in the United States. . . .

2. According to estimates of the ablest American and Chinese military men, to drive out of Manchuria the 350,000 Communists will require re-equipment of the Chinese divisions which now have worn out American arms, and also the training and equipment of ten new divisions.

In North China the problem is one of cornering guerrillas. For this purpose light-armed, fast-moving troops are needed. American and Chinese officers estimate that 20 divisions properly equipped should be able to clean up North China.

Even a small air force would greatly facilitate operations in both North China and Manchuria. We have thousands of planes which are obsolete and valueless in terms of our air force but first-rate material for the Chinese. To declassify this material and turn it over to the Chinese would cost us nothing.

The total cost to the United States of the military element in this Three-Year Plan would probably be no more than $200,000,000 a year— $600,000,000 in all. . . .

3. But all this aid will be ineffective unless the Chinese, in addition to supplying the men who fight and die, can revitalize their political life, arouse a new spirit in the country, and raise morale in the army. Can we help them to do that, or will suggestions from us be considered impertinent? They will not be, if they are made by the right man in the right way.

We have in the Far East today a general who possesses the military knowledge, political skill, and personal magnitude to organize such cooperation. If President Truman were to ask General MacArthur to add to his present duties and powers the title of Personal Representative of the President and the rank of Ambassador, and to organize with the Generalissimo a joint plan to prevent subjugation of China by the Soviet Union, the whole Far Eastern horizon would brighten with hope.

If China falls into the hands of Stalin, all Asia, including Japan, sooner or later will fall into his hands. The man power and resources of Asia will be mobilized against us. The independence of the United States will not live a generation longer than the independence of China.

Document 5-h†

Report of a Gallup Poll, April 28, 1948

(AIPO—Apr. 28, '48) Do you approve or disapprove of the United States giving the Chiang Kai-shek (Nationalist) Government more military supplies, goods, and money?

	Approve	Disapprove	No opinion
National total	55%	32%	13%
By Geographical Section			
New England and middle Atlantic	57%	31%	12%
East central	51	35	14
West central	55	32	13
South	57	26	17
Far West	52	33	15

†From: *Public Opinion Quarterly,* Fall 1948, p. 548.

6

The Policy of Non-intervention

Document 6-a†

Marshall's Views on the China Aid Act

We have had many proposals for this Government to support the Chinese military program. That is easy to say, but extraordinarily difficult and dangerous to do. It involves obligations and responsibilities on the part of this Government which I am convinced the American people would never knowingly accept. We cannot escape the fact that the deliberate entry of this country into the armed effort in China involves possible consequences in which the financial cost, though tremendous, would be insignificant when compared to the other liabilities inevitably involved. . . .

We have furnished important aid to China since V-J Day. Military aid included the transportation by U. S. facilities of Chinese Government troops from points in west China to the major cities of central and north China and from coastal points to the port of entry into Manchuria for the reoccupation of Japanese-held areas. At the end of the war the U. S. had largely equipped and partially trained 39 Chinese divisions. Additional equipment was transferred to the Chinese to complete these divisions and to replace worn-out equipment. Military lend-lease aid to the Chinese Government amounted to more than $700 million. . . . Authorized U. S. aid from V-J Day until the present date, exclusive of surplus property sales, totals $1,432,000,000, at least half of which was military assistance. . . .

All the foregoing means, at least to me, that a great deal must be done by the Chinese authorities themselves—and that nobody else can do it for them—if that Government is to maintain itself against the Communist forces and agrarian policies. It also means that our Government must be exceedingly careful that it does not become committed to a policy involving the absorption of its resources to an unpredictable extent once the obligations are assumed of a direct responsibility for the conduct of civil war in China or for the Chinese economy, or both.

There is another point that I wish to mention in consideration of this matter. There is a tendency to feel that wherever the Communist influence is brought to bear, we should immediately meet it, head on as it were. I think this would be a most unwise procedure for the reason that we would be, in

---

†From: Executive session testimony by Secretary of State Marshall before the Senate Foreign Relations Committee and the House Foreign Affairs Committee, February 21, 1948, in *The White Paper*, pp. 380-84.

effect, handing over the initiative to the Communists. They could, therefore, spread our influence out so thin that it could be of no particular effectiveness at any one point.

We must be prepared to face the possibility that the present Chinese Government may not be successful in maintaining itself against the Communist forces or other opposition that may arise in China. Yet, from the foregoing, it can only be concluded that the present Government evidently cannot reduce the Chinese Communists to a completely negligible factor in China. To achieve that objective in the immediate future it would be necessary for the United States to underwrite the Chinese Government's military effort, on a wide and probably constantly increasing scale, as well as the Chinese economy. The U. S. would have to be prepared virtually to take over the Chinese Government and administer its economic, military and governmental affairs.

Strong Chinese sensibilities regarding infringement of China's sovereignty, the intense feeling of nationalism among all Chinese and the unavailability of qualified American personnel in the large numbers required argue strongly against attempting any such solution. It would be impossible to estimate the final cost of a course of action of this magnitude. It certainly would be a continuing operation for a long time to come. It would involve this Government in a continuing commitment from which it would practically be impossible to withdraw, and it would very probably involve grave consequences to this nation by making of China an arena of international conflict. An attempt to underwrite the Chinese economy and the Chinese Government's military effort represents a burden on the U. S. economy and a military responsibility which I cannot recommend as a course of action for this Government.

On the other hand we in the Executive Branch of the Government have an intense desire to help China. As a matter of fact, I have struggled and puzzled over the situation continuously since my return. Our trouble has been to find a course which we could reasonably justify before Congress on other than emotional grounds. It has been a long struggle to concoct an economic program and clear it through the various Government agencies—the National Advisory Council, and, of course, the Budget Bureau, where they properly have to be very factual.

We are already committed by past actions and by popular sentiment among our people to continue to do what we can to alleviate suffering in China and to give the Chinese Government and people the possibility of working out China's problems in their own way. It would be against U. S. interests to demonstrate a complete lack of confidence in the Chinese Government and to add to its difficulties by abruptly rejecting its request for assistance. The psychological effect on morale in China would be seriously harmful.

We hope that the program we are presenting to Congress will assist in arresting the accelerating trend of economic deterioration to provide the Chinese Government with a further opportunity to lay the groundwork for stabilizing the situation. In these circumstances, I consider that this program of economic assistance, proposed with full recognition of all the unfavorable factors in the situation, is warranted by American interests.

Document 6-b†

The Senate Foreign Relations Committee in Executive Session

Senator George. ... As much as I sympathize with China, I am afraid that the $575 million is a complete waste of money if it is going to Chiang. It is a waste, that's all there is to it.

Senator Connally. $575 million for the whole of China is just giving the beggar at the corner a dime.

Senator Lodge. I do not even enthuse about treating it like Greece. ... We have a military commitment in Greece. It is true we are not going to send troops—probably we are not.

Senator Connally. Don't make any commitment on that.

Senator Lodge. I don't have the power to make a commitment, but Greece is obviously a very unfortunate place to try to send troops to. I don't think they would ever do it. But China is so damned big that the objections that hold true in the case of Greece don't hold true in the case of China.

The Chairman [Senator Vandenberg]. I think that is true. ...

Senator Connally. China bothers me a great deal. I doubt if you are going to do them any good unless you do give them military aid, yet I have no enthusiasm for it.

Senator Lodge. Senator, the day we send troops to China or to Russia, this country is through. There just isn't enough manpower in this country to protect China by manpower.

Senator Connally. I will vote for it, I suppose, but I think it is a waste of money because I don't think it will do any good.

Senator Lodge. I will be willing to vote to send them some money, but I'll be damned if I want to send them manpower. ...

Document 6-c‡

Further Executive Session Deliberations of the Senate Foreign Relations Committee

The Chairman [Senator Vandenberg]. Where do we go from here on China?

I think it is perfectly obvious that we cannot make any sort of a case for a China bill comparable with the case that we have made on the other one. I think it is perfectly obvious that this is essentially three cheers for the

†From: U. S., Congress, Senate, Executive session of the Committee on Foreign Relations, Historical series, 80th Cong., 2d sess., March 14, 1948, pp. 422-23.

‡From: Ibid., March 20, 1948, pp. 433-42.

Nationalist Government in the hope that it can get somewhere in the face of Communist opposition. . . .

We face here a fact, not a theory, and I suppose we might as well get it out of the way. The House is hell bent on writing military aid for China in this bill, and they are sure going to write it in. The form in which they have written it in, in my opinion as in yours, is completely impossible, because they have attached it to the Greek-Turkish bill, which carries all of the implications that are involved in the Greek-Turkish situation, which are entirely unsatisfactory to any of us.

By putting it into the Greek-Turkish bill they bring into play all of the terms of the Greek-Turkish bill which are essentially, so far as personnel is concerned, military missions and so forth. . . .

Senator Connally. . . . It seems to me that the more we monkey with this Chinese thing and send a mission over there and all that, the more danger there is that Russia will come in. She isn't going to stand for our approaching a military situation, and I agree with Senator Lodge that we can't send an army over there because that means that we are in a war: that is all there is to it.

Senator Lodge. And there is no end to it. . . .

The Chairman. . . . I come back to the fact that we have just got to coldbloodedly here deal with the fact that we confront a condition and not a theory, and half of it is parliamentary and half of it is Chinese, and I think the House is about as imponderable as China is in dealing with it.

I was about to say, though, that it is not confined to the House. We have some key men in the Senate, and the chairman of the Appropriations Committee is one of them. This is sine qua non so far as he is concerned.

Senator George. He is for China, is he?

The Chairman. And military aid.

Senator Lodge. What is the opposite of sine qua non? That's what I am. . . .

Senator George. . . . Don't you suppose the House will be reasonable about it, if we just said we have to take more time on China? I don't know. Of course you have, as you say, some people in the Senate that are going to want to do something. You don't think we could make any progress?

The Chairman. We can try, Senator. All I know is that I made a personal appeal three times to the Republican House leadership, and Senator Lodge was with me on one occasion. I laid it down just as strongly as I knew how to lay it down.

Senator George. I don't know what to say about it. I am just not willing to go along with it myself at this time, I know that. I just don't see any point in it, and I don't see any commonsense in it. . . .

Senator Hickenlooper. Mr. Chairman, that gets you down to the point that if China is in the state of collapse that Chiang indicated a couple of days ago, if they are that near the brink and you toss another $570 million in there, won't the scrounging around to get theirs be more ahead of the catastrophe than it has been in the past?

The Chairman. That is all true, Senator. There is one other factor, though, that we have not mentioned, that I do not think can be overlooked because it crops out in all the thinking of the country, and in most of the newspaper comment, and it is this basic abstraction that we are undertaking to resist Communist aggression, and we are ignoring one area completely and letting it completely disintegrate without even a gesture of assistance. . . . One House of this Congress having gone as far as it has in connection with China, suppose the whole thing failed and we didn't do anything. Wouldn't that inevitably be the end of the Nationalist Government in China forthwith? . . . Do we want that responsibility? . . .

Senator Wiley. At the same time we have to be sure we don't get our nose under the military tent so it is just one step further in.

The Chairman. We just all agree on that, Senator. . . . It seems to me our problem is to see how cheaply we can avoid the calamity to which I just recently referred; that we dare not take the responsibility for the collapse of the Nationalist Government in China. Our very practical problem is, what is the cheapest way in which we can meet that situation, because it is a condition and not a theory. . . .

Senator Wiley. What about this argument that you make that we don't want to face the responsibility of seeing Chiang go to hell? Here, we are going to have the same thing if we let him linger on for 12 months. There are other imponderables in the picture. The same argument will be thrown at us: "You had better give us this amount or we will go to hell."

Senator Hickenlooper. Maybe hell will be more attractive at the end of 12 months.

Senator Hatch. You will have your European Recovery Program 12 months past, and you will know better what the world situation is than we do today. We may all be going to hell by that time. . . .

The Chairman. I think the American people generally are deeply sympathetic with China.

Senator George. That's right.

The Chairman. And her resistance against communism even more than Europe's against communism.

Senator George. They are sympathetic. There is one way to save China from Russian communism, and that is to send an army up on the Manchurian border big enough to stop it. Otherwise you are not ever going to stop communism in China. . . .

Senator Hickenlooper. I think to give them the money and not earmark it is the only way you can do. Otherwise you are tied up with the military and it would be, as Senator George says, more than an adventure in chaos if we got into that in a military way. It would be complete chaos.

Document 6-d†

The China Aid Act, April 3, 1948

Sec. 401. This title may be cited as the "China Aid Act of 1948."

Sec. 402. Recognizing the intimate economic and other relationships between the United States and China, and recognizing that disruption following in the wake of war is not contained by national frontiers, the Congress finds that the existing situation in China endangers the establishment of a lasting peace, the general welfare and national interest of the United States, and the attainment of the objectives of the United Nations. It is the sense of the Congress that the further evolution in China of Principles of individual liberty, free institutions, and genuine independence rests largely upon the continuing development of a strong and democratic national government as the basis for the establishment of sound economic conditions and for stable international economic relationships. Mindful of the advantages which the United States has enjoyed through the existence of a large domestic market with no internal trade barriers, and believing that similar advantages can accrue to China, it is declared to be the policy of the people of the United States to encourage the Republic of China and its people to exert sustained common efforts which will speedily achieve lasting peace and prosperity in the world. It is further declared to be the policy of the people of the United States to encourage the Republic of China in its efforts to maintain the genuine independence and the administrative integrity of China, and to sustain and strengthen principles of individual liberty and free institutions in China through a program of assistance based on self-help and cooperation: Provided, That no assistance to China herein contemplated shall seriously impair the economic stability of the United States. It is further declared to be the policy of the United States that assistance provided by the United States under this title should at all times be dependent upon cooperation by the Republic of China and its people in furthering the program: Provided further, That assistance furnished under this title shall not be construed as an express or implied assumption by the United States of any responsibility for policies, acts, or undertakings of the Republic of China or for conditions which may prevail in China at any time.

Sec. 403. Aid provided under this title shall be provided under the applicable provisions of the Economic Cooperation Act of 1948 which are consistent with the purposes of this title. It is not the purpose of this title that China in order to receive aid hereunder, shall adhere to a joint program for European recovery.

Sec. 404. (a) In order to carry out the purposes of this title, there is hereby authorized to be appropriated to the President for aid to China a sum not to exceed $338,000,000 to remain available for obligation for the period of one year following the date of enactment of this Act.

(b) There is also hereby authorized to be appropriated to the President a

†From: Public Law 472, Title IV.

sum not to exceed $125,000,000 for additional aid to China through grants, on such terms as the President may determine and without regard to the provisions of the Economic Cooperation Act of 1948, to remain available for obligation for the period of one year following the date of enactment of this Act.

Sec. 405. An agreement shall be entered into between China and the United States containing those undertakings by China which the Secretary of State, after consultation with the Administrator for Economic Cooperation, may deem necessary to carry out the purposes of this title and to improve commercial relations with China.

Document 6-e†

Report from the National Security Council on Short-Term Aid

Problem

1. To assess and appraise the position of the United States regarding short-term assistance to China, taking into account the security interests of the United States.

Analysis

2. The basic long-range objective of the United States in China is the furtherance of a stable, representative government over an independent and unified China which is friendly to the United States and capable of becoming an effective barrier to possible Soviet aggression in the Far East. In view of the chaos in China, however, the most important objective which it is practicable to pursue in the short run is the prevention of complete communist control of China.

3. . . . . For the foreseeable future . . . China is likely to be poverty-stricken and technologically backward. For the United States and USSR, it possesses politico-military significance because of its (a) geographical position and (b) tremendous manpower. China's propinquity to Southeast Asia means that if the Chinese Communists take over all China, they would in time probably strengthen communist movements in Indochina, Burma, and areas further south.

4. China is torn internally by civil war between the National Government and the Chinese Communists, and is menaced on the north by Russian imperialism. The present trend in China is toward increasing instability and the extension of Communist military and political influence. Without external assistance, for which the United States is the obvious source, the National Government has little prospect of reversing or arresting this trend, because of its declining military strength, the maladministration and

---

†From: Draft report of the National SecurityCouncil on The Position of the United States regarding Short-Term Assistance to China, March 24, 1948, in *FRUS*, vol. 8, 1948, pp. 44-50.

corruption prevailing throughout its civil and military structure, its inability to cope with economic deterioration, and its lack of popular support. The principal factor operating in favor of the National Government is the prospect of United States assistance. Any improvement in the position of the Chinese National Government, therefore, requires both substantial internal reforms and foreign assistance.

5. If unchecked, present trends will lead to disintegration of the National Government's authority, decisive military successes for the Chinese Communists, the spread of warlordism, the acceleration of tendencies toward separatism and rebellion. Such disintegration would in all probability result in the eventual domination of China by the Communist party. As a last-resort alternative to disintegration the National Government might seek a compromise settlement of its conflict with the Communists. But it is inconceivable that the communists would agree to such a settlement except on terms giving them a dominating position in the government. However, in the case of either disintegration or compromise, it is probable that the acute political and economic disorganization which would result would retard the development of a Communist China as an effective instrument of Soviet policy for some years.

6. Deteriorating economic conditions are steadily weakening the political position of the National Government. In the absence of foreign aid, inflation may quickly lead to a virtually complete collapse of the national currency, thereby producing a political crisis and depriving the National Government of the means of supporting its military forces.

7. In the Chinese civil war the USSR continues to recognize the National Government, and thus far has refrained from giving overt material assistance to the Chinese Communists. It is apparent nevertheless that Soviet sympathies lie with the Chinese Communists, who are in effect an instrument for the extension of Soviet influence. So long as conditions in China continue to deteriorate according to the present pattern, which is favorable to the Chinese Communists, the USSR probably will refrain from open intervention. On the other hand to the extent that US aid tended to reverse the present course of the civil war, the USSR would probably counter by strengthening and encouraging the Chinese Communists.

8. In these circumstances the following possible courses of action are open to the United States:

a. To refrain from furnishing further economic and military assistance.

The adoption of this course would be based upon an assumption that communist expansion in China can be reversed, if at all, only at a cost greater than the United States can afford to bear. Such a course would in all probability lead to a prompt collapse of the National Government. It is not clear whether such a collapse would mean a slower communist consolidation of power. The advantage of this course is that it would make available aid for areas of greater strategic significance. On the other hand, refusal of further aid would be a reversal of past US policy and contrary to the sentiment in the United States in favor of "helping China."

b. To furnish extensive military and economic assistance in an effort to assist the National Government to defeat the Chinese Communists.

This course of action might eventually make possible a unified non-Communist China as a potential ally of the United States. The military manpower and resources of China would not be opposed to the United States in the event of war, bomber overflight of China would be free from interference by locally based aircraft, a vast area would be provided for escape and evasion tactics, and potential sites would be available for advanced airbases if desired. The announcement of firm support of the National Government by the United States would have a psychological effect which would probably be beneficial to the National Government. On the other hand, the United States would be committed to a policy involving the absorption of its resources to an unpredictable extent, once it assumed such direct responsibility for the Nationalist side of the civil war and for the Chinese economy. In view of the strong position of the Chinese Communists, the United States, in order to make this course of action effective, would have to be prepared virtually to take over the Chinese government and administer its economic, political and governmental affairs. It would be impossible to estimate the final cost of a course of action of this magnitude, which would be a continuing commitment from which it would be practically impossible to withdraw. Moreover, large-scale U. S. assistance to the National Government would probably result in large-scale Soviet assistance to the Chinese Communists. In the resultant mounting spiral of support and counter-support, the advantage would be with the USSR, because of its favorable geographical position and the vitality of the Chinese Communist movement. Such a development might lead to a Spanish-type revolution or to general hostilities.

c. To furnish limited aid to China in the form of both military and economic assistance.

State Dept. Member of the NSC Staff, concurred in by the National Security Resources Board Member of the NSC Staff

This course of action would be in the nature of buying time in China. It would not insure the defeat of the Communists nor is it likely, in the absence of resolute self-help on the part of the National Government, even to reverse the present trend of communist advance. But it might retard communist progress, enabling the National Army to continue the fight for some time to come and thereby provide the National Government with a new opportunity to attempt a stabilization of the internal situation. It would restrict the initial drain on US resources. But as it became evident that such aid was inadequate to check the communists, the limited military aid given could be represented as an obligation necessitating further military, as well as economic, commitments to China. This process could continue indefinitely and lead to deeper and deeper involvement of our national strength in an area of, at best, secondary strategic importance to us. At this critical juncture the United

States Government cannot afford thus to compromise its freedom of decision and action based upon considerations of its own vital interests.

Army, Navy, and Air Force Members of the NSC Staff

This course of action would be in the nature of buying time in China. Without immediate military assistance it is estimated that the Communists can completely consolidate their hold on Manchuria and extend their operations south of the Great Wall. Limited military aid would not insure the defeat of the Communists but would enable the National Army to continue the fight for some time thereby providing the National Government with a further opportunity to stabilize the internal situation. It might enable the National Army progressively to consolidate the control of the National Government over areas south of the Great Wall. The funds devoted to economic aid would be a much better investment in the advancement of China's economic stability if expended under reasonably stable military conditions. Such a course of action would limit the drain on United States resources, would avoid a complete underwriting of the National Government, and would not errevocably commit the United States to further assistance.

d. To furnish limited economic assistance to China.

State Dept. Member of the NSC Staff, Concurred in by the National Security Resources Board Member of the NSC Staff

Under this course of action, US military and naval missions would remain in China, but the United States Government would not directly provide military supplies. This course, in common with c above, would limit the drain on US resources and avoid a complete underwriting of the National Government. In addition, it would avoid a reaffirmation of US obligations to supply military equipment leading to renewed demands for still more military aid. This policy, nevertheless, would make it possible for the Chinese Government to acquire military equipment from US surplus and through commercial channels in the US and other countries, but in smaller quantities than under c above. The military responsibility for the survival of the National Government would be clearly placed upon Chinese shoulders.

Army, Navy, and Air Force Members of the NSC Staff

Under this course of action, US military and naval missions would remain in China, but the United States Government would not directly provide military supplies. However, the effectiveness of the US military and naval missions would be at a minimum. This course, in common with c above, would limit the drain on US resources and avoid a complete underwriting of the National Government. In addition, it would avoid a reaffirmation of US obligations to supply more military aid. Theoretically, this policy would make it possible for the Chinese Government to acquire military equipment from the US surplus and through commercial channels in the United States and other countries in smaller quantities than under c above and after much greater delay. The military responsibility for the survival of the National Government would be clearly placed upon Chinese shoulders. It is questionable that the National Government is capable of adequately discharging its responsibilities to supply its armies. The danger in such a course is the Nationalist armies might be driven from the field. Such an event leading toward communist control of China would be highly unfavorable to US prestige and interests.

Conclusions

State Dept. Member of the NSC Staff, Concurred in by the National Security Resources Board Member of the NSC Staff

9. The United States should furnish only limited economic assistance to the National Government of China on a scale designed to (a) retard economic deterioration, and (b) provide that Government with an opportunity to acquire limited military supplies with its own resources.

Army, Navy, and Air Force Members of the NSC Staff

10. The United States should furnish limited economic and military assistance to the National Government of China on a scale sufficient to retard economic and military deterioration and provide that Government with an opportunity to stabilize its internal political and military situation.

11. The United States assistance program in China should be regarded as subordinate to the efforts to stabilize conditions in areas of more strategic importance.

Document 6-f†

The Military Situation in China, June, 1948

In June 5 conference at Embassy, Badger discussed his views on present military situation in China and expressed conviction that Communist occupation Manchuria and North China would increase strategic advantage of Soviet Union in Far East to point where American interests would be threatened and to point where, in event war between Soviet Union and States, eastern defenses of Soviet would be impregnable. He also states his belief that Government armies now lack capability of preventing Communist occupation Manchuria and North China, mainly because of lack of efficient planning and effective leadership, and that provision of high level American planning staff would turn tide in favor of Nationalists. He concluded by saying that he feels it incumbent on him, by virtue of his assignment as ComNavWesPac [Commander Naval Forces Western Pacific], to report this situation to the Joint Chiefs and to recommend that an American planning staff be assigned to the Chinese Government to participate direction of the

†From: Ambassador Stuart to Secretary of State Marshall, June 9, 1948, in *FRUS*, vol. 7, 1948, pp. 282-83.

Nationalist military operations against the Communists.

On June 8 Barr received telegram from Wedemeyer requesting [Army Advisory Group] comments on military, political and economic situation and recommendations on American participation in Nationalist military effort on planning level. We believe Barr will recommend assignment American staff for operational planning and formation field teams to check on implementation of plans and gather information for planning purposes. Wedemeyer requested comments "to prepare briefing for Secretary of Army who is appearing before Senate committee."

From the above we conclude Joint Chiefs becoming concerned over deterioration Government military position in north and prospect that Communists will soon occupy North China and Manchuria. We gather that recommendations of Barr and Badger are likely to be sympathetically received by Joint Chiefs, who are aware of military significance of North China in American strategic requirements, and equally aware of fact that military shortcomings of Government are mainly along lines of failure of Nanking Supreme Staff to conceive and implement adequate plans. We are aware of implications of action suggested by Badger and Barr and agree with them that such action is necessary if deterioration situation in China is to be stopped and tide turned in our favor. Onus of establishing "field teams" suggested by Barr might be lessened by use of strategically located assistant military attaches for that purpose.

Document 6-g†

"The U. S. Government Should Not Attempt to Run the Chinese Government's War"

Secretary Forrestal opened the conversation by referring to the letter addressed to him by Senator Bridges, Chairman of the Senate Appropriations Committee, asking for information with respect to Chinese military needs and to what extent they would be met by the grants under the China Aid Act of 1948. He continued that he wished to have no conflict in what has already been said on this subject in any statements that may be made by representatives of the National Military Establishment who would testify on aid to China before the Senate Appropriations Committee. Secretary Forrestal stated that the Chinese had indicated that the $125 million grants under the China Aid Act would be used for military purchases under the following allocations among its armed services: Army, $87,500,000; Air Force, $28,000,000; and Navy $9,500,000.

Secretary Royall stated that an ad hoc committee of Army, Navy and Air Force representatives, in which General Wedemeyer participated, had estimated that Chinese Government military needs against the Communists

†From: Memorandum by Secretary of State Marshall of a conversation with Secretary of Defense Forrestal, Secretary of the Army Royall, and others, June 7, 1948, in *FRUS*, vol. 8, 1948, pp. 84-85.

for one year totalled $973,000,000, and had supported the $125 million grants provided that Chinese expenditures of these funds were supervised. He pointed out that he saw no justification for piece-meal programs which would fall short of the objective of providing realistic assistance and for that reason he did not agree that the U. S. should give military aid to China. He further said that he had so testified before the House Appropriations Committee. . . .

I pointed out that the U. S. Government must not allow itself to become undesirably involved in administering the $125 million grants and that it was necessary to maintain a distinction between advice and assistance lest the U. S. Government be placed in a position of underwriting the entire Chinese military program and running the Chinese Government. I indicated my belief that the U. S. Government should limit its action in this regard to putting the Chinese in contact with the concerned officers of the Department of the Army, Navy and Air Force who could give them help in spending these funds wisely and asked Secretary Forrestal to furnish the names of such officers so that this information could be transmitted to the Chinese Ambassador.

Secretary Forrestal said that the core of the problem seemed to be the degree of guidance which should be extended to the Chinese Government in the spending of the $125 million grants.

I again expressed the opinion that the U. S. Government should not attempt to run the Chinese Government's war but should point out the channels through which the assistance provided in these grants could best be made available. In reply to Secretary Forrestal's query whether the U. S. Government should supervise the Chinese Government's purchasing program under these grants, I stated that there was no objection to giving the Chinese appropriate advice in this regard but that the U. S. should not undertake to run the Chinese Government military effort in China.

Document 6-h†

The United States Must Not Get "Sucked In"

Referring to the recent top secret telegrams on the China situation received from General Barr and the Air Division of the U. S. Army Advisory Group, Secretary Royall said that they gave him pause for concern in that they were logical telegrams indicating the great need for control of military operations in China. . . .

I expressed the opinion that the supervision of the expenditures under the enabling act of the $125 million grants was sufficiently covered by the terms established by the President. I continued that these terms avoided a serious dilemma for the U. S. and were sufficient to protect U. S. interests. . . .

I observed that the important thing was to find out how to do this without "getting sucked in", since it was obviously the Chinese purpose so to involve the United States.

†From: Memorandum by Secretary of State Marshall of a conversation with Secretary of the Army Royall, General Bradley, General Wedemeyer, and others, June 11, 1948, in *FRUS*, vol. 8, 1948, pp. 91-99.

General Wedemeyer observed that two years ago the objectives of U. S. policy could have been achieved by such action and that one year ago a solution in north China could have been found through the use of U. S. advisers in that area, but that now there was no moral courage in the Chinese Government and it could not control its commanders. He stated that he would now hesitate to advise that U. S. advisers be placed with Chinese Army units as is being done in Greece. . . .

I expressed the opinion that it would be easy to help the Chinese Navy along the coast since that meant no real difficulties with respect to possible involvement and that we should be able to do something to assist the Chinese Air Force but that I did not know how to act on the ground side.

General Wedemeyer and General Bradley expressed doubt regarding the air phase of assistance and General Wedemeyer said that he would hesitate to go too far on the air side since the Chinese Air Force would kill more Chinese civilians than Communists. He explained that he was dubious about having U. S. personnel flying in Chinese planes and said that he had recently read an article in an American magazine describing U. S. pilots flying L-5s in some operations in China.

I pointed out that we could do something with regard to transport planes and could assist on the maintenance side and asked General Bradley what he would suggest.

General Bradley said that he would not place U. S. advisers with Chinese units as recommended by General Barr. . . .

I then asked General Wedemeyer what his reaction was.

General Wedemeyer replied that he feared that the U. S. would be blamed for the final debacle and that he would not recommend that U. S. advisers be placed with Chinese units as recommended by General Barr. He added that a Joint Chiefs of Staff directive, which had been under consideration since February 7 and had been agreed upon on June 9, approved the use of U. S. advisers in such capacity but that he thought it unwise.

Secretary Royall agreed with this view and said that he did not even think military supplies should be given to the Chinese Government. He continued that the recent telegrams from the U. S. Army Advisory Group had convinced him of the seriousness and hopelessness of the situation and of the necessity of the U. S. Government going all the way in if anything were to be accomplished. . . .

General Wedemeyer observed that while the Joint Chiefs of Staff were aware of the military side of the situation they would not know the political implications thereof and Secretary Royall said that the Joint Chiefs of Staff should reconvene and reconsider this directive. General Bradley explained that he had not been present at the Joint Chiefs of Staff meeting at which this directive was approved and that he would take steps to arrange for reconsideration of the directive. . . .

Secretary Royall concluded the discussion with the following summary of the decisions reached regarding the hearing before the Senate Appropriations Committee on June 12: "It is agreed then that General Wedemeyer and I tomorrow will say that we should take out the Greco-Turkish proviso, refer to the President's administrative terms and state that we intend to implement this part of the China Aid Act to as great an extent as possible without involvement by having the Army Advisory Group check on the deliveries of the military supplies from that end."

Document 6-i†

"Inaction Will Not Be in Our Interests"

We assume that our purposes in Far East continue best to be served by existence of political stability in China under friendly government. Trend is now in opposite direction and we must seek means to alter it. Inaction would not be in our interests.

Present regime has lost confidence of people. This is reflected in refusal of soldiers to fight and in refusal of people to cooperate in economic reforms. Government leaders are befuddled and need guidance if situation is to be saved. Accordingly, we recommend that:

We continue to support present regime to the utmost feasible in light of our commitments elsewhere and of our total resources. This would require the concentration of our military and economic aid in all-out effort to assist the Government in containing Communist armed forces within their present military boundaries. Present measures and those now planned are insufficient for the task. More bold and more imaginative measures are needed. . . . We would certainly have to go to the Generalissimo, point out the desperate situation and endeavor to impress upon him the need for drastic action, including removal of incompetents.

In addition, we should:

(a) Make strenuous efforts to find some way to reinstill into the Chinese Nationalist soldier the will to fight. This might be done by materially increasing staff of CO, JUSMAG [Commanding Officer, Joint U. S. Military Advisory Group] and giving him complete authority to extend advice of his group as far down the Chinese military command as possible after prior agreement of Generalissimo that acceptance and implementation JUSMAG advice on all military questions, including personnel, will be price of stepped-up American aid in military and other fields;

(b) Rush shipment of arms and ammunition already requisitioned. . . .

Such a course of action, even with only reasonable prospects of success, would appear to be that which is in the best interests of the U. S. Nevertheless, given our commitments elsewhere, and given the limits of our national resources, Department may well feel that our recommended course of action is impossible. Also, our military advisers feel that the Nationalist military establishment has very likely already suffered too great losses in manpower, materiel and morale to make any such effort successful. There is

†From: Ambassador Stuart to Secretary of State Marshall, October 22, 1948, in *FRUS*, vol. 7, 1948, pp. 505-7.

just no will to fight left in Nationalist forces and we can find no effective way to change the situation. A moral resurgence of Chinese will to resist Communist aggression is required and the requisite leadership just is not available. Unhappily, informed Chinese in all walks of life are bending their every effort to save their families, not their country.

Nevertheless, we feel the effort should be made as the only alternative we see is a Communist-dominated coalition. Such a coalition would confront us with the necessity of recognizing that government and making the best of it or getting out of China. . . .

Document 6-j†

Marshall Reaffirms His Decision

There is general agreement with your assumption that U. S. purposes in Far East would as in past be best served by existence of political stability in China under friendly government and U. S. policy and its implementation have been consistently directed toward that goal. However, underlying our recent relations with China have been fundamental consideration that U. S. must not become directly involved in Chinese civil war and U. S. must not assume responsibility for underwriting ChiGovt militarily and economically. Direct armed intervention in internal affairs China runs counter to traditional U. S. policy toward China and would be contrary to clearly expressed intent of Congress, which indicated that U. S. aid to China under $125 million grants did not involve use U. S. combat troops nor U. S. personnel in command Chinese troops. Public statements in Congress by leaders of Senate Foreign Relations Committee, which initiated Sec 404 (b) China Aid Act, indicated that aid to China under $125 million grants must be completely clear of implication U. S. underwriting military campaign ChiGovt since any such implication would be impossible over so vast an area.

Our China Aid Program was designed give ChiGovt breathing spell to initiate those vital steps necessary to provide framework within which base for economic recovery might be laid and essential for its survival. It was made clear that for main part solution China's problems was largely one for Chinese themselves and aid was intended give ChiGovt further opportunity take measures self-help.

General basic considerations governing our approach to China problem were set forth in my statement before Senate Foreign Relations and House Foreign Affairs Committees executive sessions, copy of which forwarded to you. U. S. Govt must be exceedingly careful that it does not become committed to a policy involving absorption of its resources to an unpredictable extent as would be case if the obligations are assumed of a direct responsibility for the conduct of civil war in China or for Chinese economy, or both. To achieve objective of reducing Chinese Communists to a

†From: Secretary of State Marshall to Ambassador Stuart, October 26, 1948, in *FRUS*, vol. 7, 1948, pp. 512-17.

completely negligible factor in China in immediate future it would be necessary for U. S. virtually to take over ChiGovt and administer its economic, military and govt affairs. Strong Chinese sensibilities regarding infringement China's sovereignty, intense feeling of nationalism among all Chinese and unavailability of qualified U. S. personnel in large numbers required argue strongly against attempting such a solution. It would be impossible estimate final cost course of action this magnitude. It certainly would be a continuing operation for long time to come. It would involve U. S. Govt in a continuing commitment from which it would practically be impossible withdraw, and it would very probably involve grave consequences this nation by making of China arena of international conflict. Present developments make it unlikely that any amount U. S. military or economic aid could make present ChiGovt capable of reestablishing and then maintaining its control throughout all China. There is little evidence that fundamental weaknesses of ChiGovt can be basically corrected by foreign aid. These considerations were set forth in my statement in Feb and they are certainly no less true under present circumstances. . . .

In summary, adoption course recommended [in your 22 Oct.] would violate all basic considerations underlying U. S. policy toward China, would involve U. S. directly in China's civil war, would commit this Govt to underwriting Chi Govt militarily and economically at a cost which it would be impossible estimate at time when U. S. has heavy commitments throughout world in connection with foreign aid programs and would not, in light appraisals situation submitted by Emb[assy] and consular offices in China over period several months, achieve its avowed objectives.

Document 6-k†

Report of Gallup Polls, December 15, 1948

(AIPO—Dec. 15, '48) Have you heard or read about the civil war in China?

	Yes	No
National total	79%	21%
By Education		
College	97%	3%
High School	86	14
Grade or no school	66	34

† From: *Public Opinion Quarterly*, Spring 1949, pp. 158-59.

(AIPO—Dec. 15, '48) Will you tell me what the status (present situation) of the war is in China today? Asked of 79% of a national sample who had heard or read of the war.

Communists gaining ground; Nationalists losing; desperate situation for Chinese Government	32%
Chinese people suffering, no food, no clothing	16
General answers; there's lots of bloodshed, people are fighting	6
Situation confused, don't know what to believe	2
Miscellaneous answers	3
Don't know	20
	79%

(AIPO—Dec. 15, '48) Do you think the fighting in China is a real threat to world peace or not? Asked of 79% of a national sample who had heard or read of the Chinese civil war.

Yes	45%
No	22
No opinion	12
	79%

(AIPO—Dec. 15, '48) Do you think the Chinese Communists take their orders from Moscow or not? Asked of 79% of a national sample who had heard or read of the Chinese civil war.

Yes	51%
No	10
No opinion	18
	79%

(AIPO—Dec. 15, '48) Would you favor or oppose sending Chiang Kai-shek's Nationalist Government about five billion dollars worth of goods and military supplies in the next year to try to keep China from going Communist? Asked of 79% of a national sample who had heard or read of the Chinese civil war.

Favor	28%
Qualified favor	4
Oppose	34
No opinion	13
	79%

(AIPO—Dec. 15, '48) Do you approve or disapprove of the United States giving the Chiang-Kai-shek (Nationalist) Government more military supplies, goods, and money? Asked last April.

Approve	39%
Disapprove	23
No opinion	10
Not questioned because unfamiliar with war	28

Part three

Bibliographic Essay

Sources

Public statements by officials of the executive branch are to be found in the weekly *Bulletin* of the Department of State. *The Public Papers of the Presidents: Harry S. Truman*, 8 vols. (Washington, D. C.: Government Printing Office, 1957-61) contains not only statements already printed in the State Department *Bulletin* but also segments of press conferences that, at the time, were either off-the-record or for background use only. Statements of members of the legislative branch may be found in the *Congressional Record* and in the printed hearings of Congressional committees. Of the latter, the most valuable for the subject of China policy are those of the Senate Appropriations Committee on the Third Supplemental Appropriation for 1948, the House Foreign Affairs Committee and Senate Foreign Relations Committee for the China Aid Act of 1948, and the Senate and House Appropriations committees for the same Act and for the European Recovery Program and the Economic Cooperation Administration. (All except the first took place during the second session of the eightieth Congress.)

For documents indicating what went on behind the scenes, there is the State Department's so-called White Paper, the proper title of which is *United States Relations with China, with Special Reference to the Period 1944-49* (Washington, D. C.: Government Printing Office, 1949; *reissued*, Stanford: Stanford University Press, 1967). It includes a sample of the State Department's files. A much larger sample from those files is now available in the State Department's historical series, *Foreign Relations of the United States* (Washington, D. C.: Government Printing Office, 1861-). Volumes 7 for 1945 (1969), 9 and 10 for 1946 (1972), 7 for 1947 (1972), and 7 and 8 for 1948 (1973) consist entirely of material on China, while other volumes for the same years contain material which is relevant to the subject. An important supplementary source in the Senate Foreign Relations Committee's *Historical Series*, which now includes transcripts of executive session hearings on the China Aid Act of 1948.

There are some other fragmentary records of American policy debates. A few extracts from President Truman's diaries appear in William Hillman, *Mr. President* (New York: Farrar, Straus, Young, and Giroux, 1952) and in Margaret Truman, *Harry S. Truman* (New York: Morrow, 1973). Extracts from the diaries of the secretary of the navy and later secretary of defense are in Walter Millis, ed., *The Forrestal Diaries* (New York: Viking, 1951) and from those of the onetime secretary of commerce in John M. Blum, ed., *The Price of Vision: The Diaries of Henry A. Wallace* (Boston: Houghton Mifflin, 1973). There are a few mentions of China in David E. Lilienthal, *Journals: The Atomic Energy Years, 1945-50* (New York: Harper and Row, 1964). Some extracts from the diary of a foreign service officer in the embassy in China appear in John F. Melby, *The Mandate of Heaven: Record of a Civil War, China 1945-49* (Toronto: University of Toronto Press, 1968).

Valuable but less reliable sources are memoirs by participants in the policy debates. The more important are Harry S. Truman, *Memoirs*, 2 vols., (Garden City, N. Y.: Doubleday, 1955-56); James F. Byrnes, *Speaking Frankly* (New York: Harper and Brothers, 1947) and *All in One Lifetime* (New York: Harper, 1958); Dean G. Acheson, *Present at the Creation* (New York: W. W. Norton, 1969); George F. Kennan, *Memoris, 1925-50* (Boston: Little, Brown, 1967); Albert C. Wedemeyer, *Wedemeyer Reports!* (New York: Henry Holt, 1958); and John Leighton Stuart, *Fifty Years in China* (New York: Random House, 1954). Casting some sidelight on the perspectives of others in the field are *A Secret War: Americans in China, 1944-45* (Carbondale: Southern Illinois University Press, 1964) by Oliver J. Caldwell, a former O.S.S. agent; *China Assignment* (Seattle: University of Washington Press, 1964) by Karl L. Rankin of the consular corps; *The Amerasia Papers: Some Problems in the History of U. S.-China Relations* (Berkeley: University of California Press,

1971) by John Stewart Service; and John Paton Davies, *Dragon by the Tail* (New York: W. W. Norton, 1972), a history *cum* memoir by a foreign service-officer China specialist who offended Hurley, was therefore transferred, and as a result, watched the post-1945 Chinese scene from the vantage point of Moscow. Arthur N. Young, *China and the Helping Hand, 1937-1945* (Cambridge, Mass.: Harvard University Press, 1963) is an analytical work by an American who returned to China in 1946 as an economic adviser to Chiang.

Some source material of the same character as that in memoirs is to be found in retrospective testimony elicited during later congressional hearings. There is testimony relating to 1945-49 China policy given by Marshall, Acheson, and Wedemeyer in 82nd Congress, first session, Senate Armed Services and Foreign Relations committees, "Hearings on the Military Situation in the Far East" (usually referred to as the MacArthur hearings) and by Eugene H. Dooman, John Carter Vincent, and Admiral Charles M. Cooke in 81st Congress, first and second sessions, Senate Committee on the Judiciary, Internal Security Subcommittee, "Hearings on the Institute of Pacific Relations."

Studies

The first work to attempt a systematic analysis of American China policy was the State Department "White Paper." In addition to documents, it included a 409-page narrative prepared by China specialists and historians on the State Department staff. In general, the narrative sought to demonstrate that American representatives in China and policy makers in Washington had not been sympathetic to the Communists; that they had, however, reported candidly on the immensity of the task confronting Chiang and the weakness, corruptness, and ineptitude of his regime; that they had devised and carried out programs to aid him; but that he had rejected American advice and squandered his resources. The secretary of state's foreword asserted that China had fallen to the Communists because of forces internal to China and beyond the control of the United States, and most of the text was congruent with this proposition.

The "White Paper" was designed in part to still partisan charges that Chiang had been deliberately sacrificed by pro-Communists in the government. It failed to do so. Indeed, the charges became increasingly loud. A number of Americans became persuaded that, at the very least, there had been some Communist sympathizers in the State Department; that they had gulled others into believing that the Chinese Communists were not true Communists but merely "agrarian reformers;" that they succeeded in doing this in part because Truman's advisers on foreign policy were mostly members of the eastern establishment who paid attention to Europe more than to Asia; and that, as a result, the government failed to do for Chiang what it did for anti-Communists in Europe and the Middle East.

This interpretation had its greatest currency in the early 1950s. In part, this was because American and Chinese Communist soldiers were then killing one another in Korea, and Americans were adjusting to the double shock of suddenly perceiving Chinese as enemies rather than friends and of discovering that they could be as able fighters as the Japanese had been. In part, it was because much of the nation was then in the grip of paranoid hysteria, and otherwise sensible people were sponsoring or acquiescing in witch-hunts, purges, and other excesses aimed at identifying and rooting out potential subversives.

After the Korean War, when passion and hysteria ebbed, the thesis ceased to be so widely believed. It continued to find expression in right wing publications, and it was developed in one book that pretended to be a serious history: Anthony Kubek, *How the Far East Was Lost: American Policy and the Creation of Communist China, 1941-1949* (Chicago: Henry Regnery, 1963).

Scholarly writing, as opposed to political journalism, tended throughout to accept the interpretation put forward in the "White Paper." This interpretation had been foreshadowed in the final chapter of the masterful and highly influential survey by Professor John K. Fairbank of Harvard, *The United States and China* (Cambridge, Mass.: Harvard University Press, 1948). It was incorporated more fully in later editions; and it also appeared in the standard textbooks on American diplomatic history by Professors Thomas A. Bailey of Stanford, Samuel F. Bemis of Yale, and Julius W. Pratt of Buffalo.

In 1953 there appeared the first serious monograph offering information and analysis not to be found in the "White Paper." This was *The China Tangle: The American Effort in China from Pearl Harbor to the Marshall Mission* (Princeton: Princeton University Press, 1953) by Herbert Feis. An economic historian by training and for many years the economic adviser to Secretary of State Cordell Hull, Feis had secured access to unpublished documents in the Department of State, the Department of the Army, and the Roosevelt Library. On the basis of these documents, Feis reconstructed much more fully than had the "White Paper" the record of wartime dealings with Chiang. Though his narrative trailed off after the death of Roosevelt and ended altogether at the end of 1945, it argued, in effect, that the best chance of salvation for the Nationalists had been sacrificed well before 1945, when Chiang balked at letting Wedemeyer's predecessor, General Joseph W. Stilwell, train and equip Chinese soldiers to fight the Japanese and integrate Nationalist and Communist troops into a professional national army. This thesis was documented even more fully in the three-volume official history of the China Theater: Riley Sunderland and Charles F. Romanus, *Stilwell's Mission to China* (Washington, D.C.: Office of the Chief of Military History, 1953), *Stilwell's Command Problems* (*id.*, 1955), and *Time Runs Out in C.B.I.* (*id.*, 1959). It was subsequently presented in a superbly narrated biography: Barbara W. Tuchman, *Stilwell and the American Experience in China, 1911-1945* (New York: Macmillan, 1971).

Largely owing to the scarcity of source material, the postwar history of U. S. China policy received little scholarly attention. The principal work was Tang Tsou, *America's Failure in China, 1941-1950* (Chicago: University of Chicago Press, 1963). A political scientist who was a disciple of Hans Morgenthau, Tang Tsou judged American policy to have lacked "realism." Americans had erected a mythology about China, he argued, which led them to assign it greater importance than it deserved. At the same time, they were unwilling or unable to commit to China economic and military resources which achievement of their objectives would necessarily have required. His contention was that the Truman administration should either have redefined its goals or, as in Europe, developed the wherewithal to attain them. In effect, Tang Tsou presented a modified version of the thesis in the "White Paper" and in Marshall's testimony during the MacArthur hearings. The rescue of Chiang, while not necessarily beyond American capabilities, was beyond the resources which Americans were actually prepared to use for the purpose. Based on exhaustive use of then-available printed sources, Tang Tsou's book served as a standard narrative account, even for those who did not necessarily accept its interpretation.

The late 1960s saw the flowering of a "revisionist" historiography regarding the origins and early history of the Cold War. The general guidelines for this "revisionism" had been set down in William Appleman Williams's seminal *The Tragedy of American Diplomacy* (New York: World Publishing Co., 1959; revised ed., New York: Delta Books, 1962). Williams had put forth the thesis that the United States had consistently given priority to finding markets for American capitalists. Its policy had been "open door imperialism." Pursuing this policy, it had sought to push back socialism in Europe, thus forcing the Soviet Union into defensive action. The Cold War was, in other words, of American manufacture. In developing this thesis, Williams paid almost no attention to China as a problem for the American government. He said, in effect, that the Chinese people turned to communism and that there was nothing which the United States could have done to arrest Communist success.

Most "revisionist" literature imitates Williams by paying relatively little attention to China. The principal exception is Gabriel Kolko and Joyce Kolko, *The Limits of Power: The World and United States Foreign Policy, 1945-1954* (New York: Alfred A. Knopf, 1972). Devoting two chapters of their book to China policy, the Kolkos argue that the United States did not make an all-out effort to save Chiang because American capitalists saw the Nationalists as not much better than the Communists. Since Chiang had plans for nationalizing certain industries and exercising controls over foreign investment and trade, the United States did not think it worthwhile to expend much effort in order to keep him in power. (As indicated in my preface to this volume, I find their argument unconvincing.)

There has recently begun to appear some serious monographic writing which echoes neither the old polemics about who "lost" China nor the newer polemics of "revisionists." Russell D. Buhite, *Patrick J. Hurley and American Foreign Policy* (Ithaca: Cornell Press, 1973) draws upon Hurley's private papers to make Hurley at least a more comprehensible figure. Now that official documents and private papers have begun to open, we can expect a series of monographs gradually building for us a new understanding of these still dimly understood events.

Apart from writings on governmental policy, there are four important works which touch on public opinion. Ross Y. Koen, *The China Lobby in American Politics* (New York: Macmillan, 1960), while devoted mostly to post-1949 propaganda activities, provides much information about the strongly pro-Nationalist elements among the American public. Harold R. Isaacs, *Images of Asia: American Views of China and India* (New York: Capricorn Books, 1962) and Anthony T. Steele, *The American People and China* (New York: McGraw Hill, 1964), though both focused on a later period, describe the earlier state of public knowledge and understanding concerning China. Kenneth E. Shewmaker, *Americans and Chinese Communists* (Ithaca: Cornell University Press, 1971) deals objectively and analytically with the Americans who reported on the Communists from the 1930s to the end of World War II.

Warren I. Cohen, *America's Response to China: An Interpretative History* (New York: John Wiley, 1971) is a perceptive general history, written with judiciousness and with understanding of Chinese as well as American perspectives.

Although sources on the Chinese side have been and remain relatively scarce, some noteworthy efforts have been made to assess what was going on in the Nationalist and Communist camps. In *Across the Pacific: An Inner History of American-East Asian Relations* (New York: Harcourt Brace and World, 1967), Akira Iriye delineates and compares American, Chinese Nationalist, and Chinese Communist perceptions of what happened in East Asia during and after World War II. Lionel Max Chassin, *The Communist Conquest of China: A History of the Civil War, 1945/1949* (Cambridge,

Mass.: Harvard University Press, 1965) is a penetrating analysis by a French officer who observed the conflict. It is amplified in some respects by F. F. Liu, *A Military History of Modern China, 1924-1949* (Princeton: Princeton University Press, 1956). Graham Peck, *Two Kinds of Time: A Personal History of China's Crash into Revolution* (Boston: Houghton Mifflin, 1950) was an early effort at detached analysis of the reasons for the Nationalists' defeat. Chalmers A. Johnson, *Peasant Nationalism and Communist Power: The Emergence of Revolutionary China* (Stanford: Stanford University Press, 1962) was a later one. Both are thought-provoking. For the Communist side, the most notable studies are Jerome Ch'en, *Mao and the Chinese Revolution* (New York: Oxford University Press, 1965) and Samuel B. Griffith II, *The Chinese People's Liberation Army* (New York: McGraw Hill, 1967). James P. Harrison, *The Long March to Power: A History of the Chinese Communist Party, 1921-1971* (New York: Praeger, 1972) is a lively general history. The most recent and best-documented work is Richard C. Thornton, *China: The Struggle for Power* (Bloomington: Indiana University Press, 1974).

On the perspective of the Soviet Union, Max Beloff, *Soviet Policy in the Far East, 1944-1951* (London: Oxford University Press, 1953) and Charles B. McLane, *Soviet Policy and the Chinese Communists 1931-1946* (New York: Columbia University Press, 1958) are important for background. Adam B. Ulam, *Expansion and Coexistence: The History of Soviet Foreign Policy, 1917-67* (New York: Praeger, 1968) sets Stalin's China policy in context. New information on Soviet policy has, however, recently begun to come to light. The best guidance to it is to be found in V. I. Glunin *et al.*, *Noveishaya Istoriya Kitaya, 1917-1970 gg.* (Moscow: Institut Dal'nego Vostoka, Akademii Nauk USSR, 1972). A description of British perspectives, largely based on parliamentary debates, is Brian Porter, *Britain and the Rise of Communist China, 1945-1954* (London: Oxford University Press, 1967).

For relatively up-to-date analyses of historiography, amplifying what appears here, an interested reader should turn to the essays by James Peck and Robert Dallek in *American-East Asian Relations: A Survey*, edited by Ernest R. May and James C. Thomson, Jr., (Cambridge, Mass.: Harvard University Press, 1972).

Index